EVERTON GREATS

EVERTON GREATS

KEN ROGERS

SPORTSPRINT PUBLISHING EDINBURGH
IN ASSOCIATION WITH
THE *LIVERPOOL ECHO*

ISBN 0 85976 274 2

Our thanks to the *Liverpool Echo* for assistance with pictures,
and to the many distinguished players, officials
and friends of Everton Football Club
for their help in the preparation of this book.

Phototypeset by Beecee Typesetting Services
Printed in Great Britain by Bell & Bain Ltd., Glasgow

Contents

CHAPTER ONE

Introduction

Everton's magnificent Bellefield training ground is the inner sanctum that every fan would like to penetrate in the days leading up to a big game.

Who wouldn't like to be a fly on the wall in the manager's office or the coaches' room, listening to Colin Harvey discussing team matters with his backroom team?

When I was asked to produce this book on *Everton Greats*, Bellefield seemed a symbolic place to open the great debate. My challenge was not to come up with a definitive list of all-time Goodison super heroes, but rather to present a very personal salute to some of the outstanding characters I have had the pleasure of watching — and in most cases meeting — during four highly contrasting decades.

If the Fifties were barren in terms of major honours, the Sixties were comparatively glorious. The Seventies promised much, but produced little, while the Eighties will be remembered as the era of the great Goodison renaissance.

But whether trophies have been in the cabinet or not, Everton have always had players of the very highest calibre. Down the years, the Blues have not so much produced great stars as living legends, immortal centre-forward William Ralph 'Dixie' Dean being the king of them all.

It's significant that my list of players is top heavy with forwards. Everton have always believed that attack is the best form of defence, which is why Goodison Park was tagged the 'School of Soccer Science'.

Evertonians will tell you that class is more important than clout.

When I scanned the never-ending list of candidates for this book, the problem was not so much who to put in as who to leave out. It was like trying to edit the dictionary into a sentence of manageable proportions. In other words, it was virtually impossible.

I finally settled on ten names, endeavouring to bridge all four decades. With that in mind, I restricted myself to just one current Everton player.

In doing so, I was forced to leave out such outstanding candidates as Graeme Sharp and Kevin Ratcliffe, important figures in the club's Eighties revival. So be it.

For the time being, I make no apology in revealing my Everton Greats . . . Dave Hickson, Ray Wilson, Alex Young, Brian Labone, Alan Ball, Colin Harvey, Howard Kendall, Bob Latchford, Andy Gray and Neville Southall.

These names suggest that it is possible to achieve greatness in any area of the field, be it goalkeeper, full-back, centre-back, midfielder or striker. Two of my 'Greats' played their part in England's glorious 1966 World Cup triumph. Another never won a major medal — his greatest hour coming in the Second Division — but his impact on the fans was such that no one would dare deny him a place in the Goodison Hall of Fame.

My list includes a great Corinthian, a Merseyside 'God' and possibly the most modest superstar the game has ever seen. But before I salute them in a very individual manner, let me invite you into that inner sanctum at Bellefield, courtesy of manager Colin Harvey, his assistant Terry Darracott and coach Mike Lyons, men who have sweated blood on the playing and coaching side for Everton down the years . . . blue blood, of course!

You can be that fly on the wall as we take a nostalgic journey back in time along the banks of the royal blue Mersey . . . cue for a song?

CHAPTER TWO

Inside Information

Evertonians don't come any bigger than Colin Harvey. The Goodison boss first started watching the Blues in the mid-Fifties. His father and grandfather were both avid supporters and so it wasn't long before Colin was indoctrinated into the cause, cheering on his first hero, Dave Hickson. He recalls that while the club didn't have a top team at that time, he still looked on certain individuals as great players.

He said: 'Dave fell into this category. He was blond which immediately made him stand out, and while he wasn't noted for his football ability, he was one of the bravest centre-forwards I have ever seen. The crowd loved him.

'I can remember him playing in one match and going off covered in blood. He had stitches in a nasty head wound, but returned to the field to score the winner — with his head, of course! In terms of football ability, inside-forward Wally Fielding was another player from that era who I always enjoyed watching. He was a tremendous passer of the ball and was one of my heroes at that time.

'By the time the Sixties came round, I was involved with the club myself. Bobby Collins made an impact on everyone because he was such a smashing player and a tremendous competitor. If you stepped out of line in training, then he would do you, no danger, but having said that, you looked up to him because of his ability.'

Harvey would eventually become a household name himself in the Sixties and early Seventies before embarking on a coaching career that led, almost inevitably, to the Goodison Park hot seat.

One of his early team mates was legendary forward Alex Young, or the 'Golden Vision' as he became known after a famous television play. Like Hickson, he was blond, but the similarity ends there. Hickson was the bull, ready to run through a brick wall for Everton. Young was the supreme artist, the ultimate entertainer.

Harvey said: 'Yes, he was a fantastic footballer with a brilliant touch and a great perception of the game.

'He did have a ruthless streak in him, but not many spectators were aware of it. He will always be remembered for his remarkable skill. Alex could chip a ball over you from a couple of yards away and while he wasn't very tall, his timing was such that he won things in the air that should never have been his.

'He wasn't an outgoing character, but he had an aura about him. I remember a European Cup Winners Cup tie against Real Zaragoza in November, 1966. The tie bubbled over and finished in a free-for-all with players fighting all over the pitch. Alex was so right in everything he did that he was up on his toes and adopting the old boxers' stance while everybody else lashed out with boots flying everywhere. Looking back, it was hilarious.'

Terry Darracott recalls that Young never lost his appetite for turning on the style. He said: 'I played in what was possibly one of his last games in an Everton shirt. It was a reserve match. I was 16 at the time and we played at Nottingham Forest. I was right-back and Alex was playing on the right-hand side of midfield, or right wing as it was then.

'It was quite an occasion to play alongside 'Youngy' because he was an idol to us all. Before we went out he said to me, 'Son, every time you get the ball, the first thing you must try to do is give it to me. I don't care if it's a free-kick, a throw-in or a corner, give it to me and I'll get on with it.'

'We won that game and later Alex was kind enough to take me home. When we arrived, all my mates were waiting for me in the street. I was the top man in our road for the next couple of weeks because I had actually been in

Jimmy Gabriel . . . in full flight against Wolves.

the Golden Vision's car. That's how much of an idol he
was. He drove off not realising what he had done, but he
had made my day.'

Young's attacking partner in the 1963 Championship
side was skipper Roy Vernon.

Harvey recalls: 'Vernon was a great goalscorer and a
deadly penalty taker. He had a deceptive change of pace
and, for such a slight man, was a great striker of the ball.
These days you often get two big centre-forwards. Young
and Vernon were not that type at all, but they scored a lot
of goals between them, even though they didn't
particularly like each other off the pitch.'

Harvey began to establish himself in the Everton side
the season after that 1962/63 Championship triumph. His
debut was to come in the most testing of circumstances in
the famous San Siro Stadium in Milan, playing in the
European Cup against Italian giants Inter. He was only 18,
but came to terms with the challenge like a seasoned
professional. Terry Darracott was still a schoolboy at that
time and admits that Harvey was his favourite player.

He explained: 'The local pub where my mum and dad
used to go for a drink was run — and still is — by Colin's
uncle, an Irishman called Pat Bow. All those years ago, I
was Pat Bow's runner.

'I used to go and queue for his tickets for the big games
at Goodison. The queues used to stretch for miles then and
Pat, running a lucrative business at the Bay Horse, didn't
have time to go. He would ask my mum and dad if I could
do it and I was always happy to oblige, knowing it was
Colin's uncle.

'Pat used to give me a few bob, but I didn't care about
that. I thought I was doing a favour for Colin Harvey. When
I eventually joined Everton myself, Pat told me to mention
his name to Colin. Our friendship picked up from there,
right from day one.'

Terry signed on in 1966 and his early memories are of
Young, Vernon, Brian Labone and Brian Harris. He said:

Goodbye Goodison . . . Bobby Collins waves farewell to Everton, leaving Lime Street Station to join Leeds United.

'There were some fantastic stars around then, some real household names. Being around players like that was a great learning thing for me. I was a very lucky young lad.

'I say to kids these days, 'Feel happy that you are able to train and play with good players.'

'I was brought up with a group of individuals who were not only tremendous performers out on the pitch, but also good influences off the park. People like Colin, Alan Ball and Jimmy Gabriel were absolutely fantastic in that way. If we ever did anything extra in the afternoon, which we often did in those days, you could bet your boots that one of these three, if not all of them, would come back in and join in with us, just for the sake of doing a couple of hours' extra training.

'If, as a kid, you don't pick up on things like that, then there's something wrong with you.'

When Terry mentioned Gabriel, I could only shrug. My heart told me to pick him in my *Everton Greats* because he was such a larger than life character out on the pitch. The fact that he just missed out in the final reckoning doesn't make him any less a Goodison giant. It just emphasises the quality of the candidates.

Colin Harvey tells a nice story about the powerhouse half-back who arrived from Dundee for £30,000 in March, 1960, going on to make 300 rock-solid appearances for the Blues.

He said: 'Gabby was a smashing fella and an incredible all-round competitor. The crowd loved him and he loved the crowd. He always looked after the youngsters in the team. I can remember being whacked off the ball in one particular game.

'The first one over to me was Gabby, wanting to know who the culprit was. I said 'I think it was the left-back.'

'Five minute later, the defender who had punched me was laid out flat. I'm not saying it was the right thing to do, but Gabby wouldn't have reacted if the fella hadn't stepped out of line in the first place. He simply made a point of protecting the younger lads in the side.

'Equally, he was a very good player who was happy to play football if that was the way the game was going.'

Terry Darracott was another Gabriel fan. He said: 'If a team was to get through on fighting spirit, he was the one leading the charge. No matter how the game was going to be played, Jimmy could handle it. If it was going to be a real football match with no nonsense going on, he was happy in that company.

'If things changed and you had to roll your sleeves up and get stuck in, he would still be the top man. Jimmy was very fierce, even at the training ground. When I look at training then and the way it is today, we encourage players not to make heavy challenges now for obvious reasons. You don't want key men getting injured.

Mike Lyons . . . the man who would run through a brick wall for Everton.

'I can't imagine saying to Jimmy Gabriel all those years ago: 'Gabby, watch your tackling.'

'He would have kicked the manager, the coach or who-ever for saying it. I always remember when Jimmy decided to take his coaching badge. I was an apprentice at the time and he used us as guinea pigs to coach in a session. He was even frightening doing that. I suppose there are different ways of putting things over.

'Jimmy was always a Bill Shankly type in that respect with the gravelly Scots voice. It wasn't a gentle: 'Come on lads, let's see if we can get it right.'

'It was a very different manner, but we knew Jimmy was in charge and we made sure we got it right.'

Everton had a lot of very competitive players in the Sixties, none more inspirational than Alan Ball, a cocky, supremely confident individual who marched into Goodison in 1966 and immediately stamped his mark on the place. It said everything about the manager of the day, Harry Catterick, that he chose to pay a then British record fee of £110,000 for the Blackpool player, even though Everton were on the crest of a wave after beating Sheffield Wednesday in the F.A. Cup Final. Catterick was clearly not going to rest on his laurels. Nor was Ball who breezed in, fresh from his World Cup triumph with England.

Both men were ambitious to the point of being ruthless. Colin Harvey recalls Ball's early days. He said: 'His book was called *Ball of Fire* and that was just about right. He was all sparks and action. Alan would get brought down and be up and off again in a flash. He would take his own free-kick, knock it two yards, get it back and be in full flight again before the opposition knew what was happening.

'On the day he arrived, he marched in and immediately took centre-stage. He didn't just walk into the room and sit in the corner to find his feet which would have been the case with most new players. His first words were, 'When is the lads' night-out?'

'When it came to football, he was so good at everything he did, you wanted to match him and it brought out the best in you because of it.'

Ball, Harvey and Howard Kendall linked together to form an outstanding midfield partnership, the engine room of Everton's 1970 Championship side. Ball was the kind of individual who would have a go at anything.

Harvey remembers an occasion when the Blues were playing at Newcastle and stopped off at Gosforth. He said: 'There was a little dog track close by. We went over after our evening meal for a bit of air and the racing had just begun. It was one of those events in which the winning dog could be bought. Bally snapped it up on the spot!

The unmistakable smile of Wally Fielding.

'His mate, who had travelled up on the Friday night, just to watch the game the following day, had to go home with the greyhound. It was called Filthy McNasty which must have appealed to Bally's sense of humour. After that, we used to call his poor mate McNasty. The dog actually won a few races at the flapping tracks around Bolton.

'I'll never forget the incident. It said everything about Alan Ball. It was all or nothing with him.'

Terry Darracott believes the England midfielder was the complete professional.

He said: 'Alan was a leader. He was a brilliant ball player, he scored goals and he created them — and he made the players around him feel ten feet tall.'

Sitting in that Bellefield inner sanctum, listening to Harvey and Darracott bubbling about some of the great Goodison characters of the past, was a treat. I was brought up in the district of Everton, attending Major Lester Primary School on Everton Valley which is no more than a goal kick away from both Goodison Park and Anfield.

These days I report on Everton AND Liverpool for the *Liverpool Echo,* hopefully in a totally unbiased manner. As a lad — and in keeping with all Merseyside kids — I had no divided loyalties.

I was a soccer mad 14-year-old when the Blues won the title in 1963, watching most of the home games that year from the paddock — a favourite 'spec' for a certain Mike Lyons.

Like Colin and Terry, he was a loyal fan long before he became an integral part of the club as a player and a coach. He said: 'From eight onwards, my dad used to take me to every home game with my brother Joseph.

'We sat in the Gwladys Street stand at first, but I switched to the paddock in time for that 1962/63 campaign after getting a season ticket for Christmas. My favourite player was always Jimmy Gabriel because he would have a right good go in every game. I got my confirmation name 'James' because of Gabby. My brother named his son 'Alex' after Young. It's fair to say that we are all big Evertonians.'

As a kid, Mike was always first in the ground on Saturdays. He remembers that 62/63 season vividly, recalling the day when he nearly missed out on one of the most important matches of the year, the home clash against Tottenham in April.

Mike said: 'It was the day when we effectively took control of the Championship. I got there early as usual, but I couldn't find my season ticket. I was in tears and ran back to the main road to catch a bus home. My dad had already left so I bombed back down to Goodison, still without my ticket.

'The turnstile operator must have recognised me as the

A man who enjoys his work . . . Everton coach Terry Darracott.

kid who always got there early because he agreed to let me in.'

Mike had ticket trouble again when Everton reached the F.A. Cup Final in 1968, using his initiative when desperation set in on Wembley Way. He vaulted the turn-stiles and raced out onto the terraces — only to find himself in the middle of the West Brom hordes! His misery was compounded when Jeff Astle thundered home a lone goal winner to secure Albion the Cup.

One of the great characters of the Sixties was goal-keeper Gordon West. He was a bundle of laughs as well as being one of the country's leading keepers. Mike recalls that the club apprentices and the young reserves were all terrified of 'Westy' — not least when he decided to hold court at Bellefield.

He said: 'In those days we would finish at 11.30 on Friday mornings and then have to wait a couple of hours until manager Harry Catterick put the teams up. We had four sides all playing on the Saturday in those days — first team, reserves, 'A' team and 'B' team. To help kill the boredom of hanging around, 'Westy' would preside over us with a mop on his head, inventing a variety of court cases.

'One of the young lads was 'tried' for being a mummy's boy. His crime was that he was getting dropped off by his mother every morning when all the other lads had to get the bus to work. The punishments, if found guilty, seem cruel now, but it was all part of the business of growing up.

'You could be thrown into a cold bath or be forced to lie on the floor, 12 of your team mates piling on top for the 'crusher' treatment.

'On a trip to Singapore, 'Westy' decided to organise midnight sprint races down the hotel corridor. It was a typical stunt. His room mate was always captain and centre-half Brian Labone. To the younger lads, Brian seemed to be like the village squire because he owned a race horse and was the leader we all looked up to.'

The Evertonians loved West who was the master of the angles and brilliant when it came to instinctive saves. The Goodison faithful have always had a very special affinity with the game's great entertainers.

My fascinating Bellefield debate was drawing to a close. Colin Harvey, Terry Darracott and Mike Lyons had proved to be informative and inspirational company.

It was time to get down to brass tacks . . . and my own EVERTON GREATS.

CHAPTER THREE

Dave Hickson

When Dave Hickson went to war on the football field, opposing centre-halves sent for their tin helmets and dug in for a mighty battle.

The blond centre-forward, the all-action Cannonball Kid of the Fifties and early Sixties, has the distinction of having played for all three Merseyside League clubs . . . Everton, Liverpool and Tranmere Rovers.

But it is in the royal blue of Everton that Dave enjoyed the best days of a remarkable, often stormy career. His swashbuckling style, his courage, his will to win and his single-minded approach to every game he played in, made him a firm favourite with the Goodison Park fans.

Elation in the F.A. Cup. Dave Hickson is chaired off after scoring Everton's winner in the sixth round against Aston Villa in 1953.

The Liverpudlians hated him until the day he crossed the Park in November, 1959, for the princely sum of £12,000. The man the Anfield hordes had christened 'Dirty Dave' scored twice on his debut in a red shirt and suddenly he was a super hero in their eyes as well.

Someone once wrote: 'Hickson was not built for finesse, nor particularly did he try to cultivate it. He had fire in his nostrils.'

Dave played to win and it often got him into trouble with referees. So much so that when he was sitting in a train compartment at Lime Street Station at the height of his fame and the guard's whistle blew, the centre-forward popped his head out of the window and enquired 'What have I done now ref?'

Such Hickson stories are legendary. The man only had one purpose in life . . . to stick the ball in the back of the net. He scored 111 goals in 243 appearances for Everton, going in where it hurts to win an army of admirers.

Dave was born in Salford and had a leaning to Manchester United as a boy, but his family moved to Ellesmere Port where he very quickly made an impression at Schoolboy level.

He was playing for Ellesmere Port Town when Everton scout Tom Corley spotted his potential, inviting him across the river to attend trials. If Dave had any doubts about joining the Blues, they were quickly dispelled by the greatest player ever to pull on an Everton shirt, the legendary William Ralph 'Dixie' Dean.

Young Hickson found himself playing for the Cheshire Army Cadets under the astute guidance of the immortal Dean. Dave said: 'I got my heading strength from Dixie. He helped me a lot at that time and we developed a great friendship.'

Dean, of course, is the man whose astonishing 60-goal haul during the 1927/28 season still stands as the all-time Football League scoring record. Dixie remained a fervent Evertonian throughout his life and was clearly a tremendous influence on Hickson at that time.

The blond number nine finally signed professional forms for the Blues in 1948, but his career was nipped in the bud almost immediately when he was called up by the Army. He finished up in Egypt and so two years of his career were effectively wiped out.

Dave said: 'It was all very frustrating because it meant that I had to come back and start all over again, but I scored five in a reserve game against Sheffield Wednesday during the 1950-51 season and went with the first team a couple of times as twelfth man.'

Hickson didn't get a game that year, even though Everton were stumbling from one disaster to another. It was the campaign in which the Blues were relegated for the first time in their history. Dave desperately wanted to do something to try and keep them up, but he didn't break into the first team until five games into the following season, making his debut at Leeds United in place of Harry Catterick, the man who would later become one of the greatest manager's Everton have ever had.

Dave said: 'We won 2-0, Tommy Eglington getting both goals. I got off the mark in a 3-3 home draw with Rotherham and I was on my way.'

Hickson plundered a creditable 14 League goals from 31 games that first season, but his elation at making the breakthrough into the senior ranks was tempered by Everton's failure to gain promotion at the first attempt.

The Blues finished seventh, but went into the 1952/53 season with a lot of confidence. It was to be a sensational year, but not on the League front. The team never got higher than seventh and finished a disappointing 16th, but they came to within an ace of claiming an F.A. Cup Final place against Blackpool.

Hickson scored two in a 3-2 third-round win over Ipswich Town. His partner John Willie Parker won all the headlines at the next hurdle with a double in a comprehensive 4-1 victory over Nottingham Forest.

The tie that followed remains one of the most memorable Cup clashes to have graced Goodison Park.

The result was satisfying enough . . . Everton 2, Manchester United 1. But it was the manner in which it was achieved that captured the hearts and minds of every supporter in the ground, and on the final whistle the name of just one man was on everybody's lips — Dave Hickson.

In the first half-hour the visitors had been slightly the better team. Jack Rowley gave United the lead after 27 minutes and the faint-hearted thought that was the end for Everton because the Manchester outfit had been one of the best teams in the country for six years.

Then George Cummins and Hickson made an opportunity which Tommy Eglington took with his right foot to equalise. The crowd roared their delight, but just before the interval Hickson was led off with a badly cut eyebrow and it looked as if he wouldn't be able to do much in the second half.

Blood was streaming down his face, but he got on with the job in hand as if his very life depended on it. The *Liverpool Echo* columnist that night reported: 'Never in my whole life have I seen a player perform with such guts as Davie showed. Twice the referee suggested he should go off.

'The player simply waved him aside and his bravery and persistence paid off after 63 minutes. Eglington squared a pass to Hickson. He appeared to have little chance, with two men in attention, but he beat one, side-stepped the other and screwed an oblique shot into the back of the net.'

Dave recalls: 'The spirit of the whole side was fantastic. I suppose that's the game many people remember me for. I had five stitches inserted over my right eye and came back on to score the winner. Another ball came over and I got in a header that hit the post. My eye split open again and there was blood all over the place. It didn't matter. The victory took us into the quarter finals and I was fortunate enough to score the only goal of the match at Aston Villa.'

Fans who were at Villa Park that day remember the effort as an absolute cracker. It actually followed a mêlée in the Everton goal, the ball being hacked clear. It went to

A welcome refresher for Dave Hickson after scoring Everton's winner against Aston Villa in February, 1953.

Hickson near the touchline, just inside the Blues' half. He played it up to Buckle who was in the outside-left position and raced forward like a man possessed to take the return pass. The centre-forward held off a Villa challenge before ramming the ball home.

On the final whistle, a crowd of about 200 people chaired and cheered Hickson all the way to the touchline. His bravery and determination, backed up by some excellent performances from the likes of Peter Farrell, Tommy Eglington and Tommy T.E. Jones, had carried the Goodison outfit to within shouting distance of the twin towers of Wembley.

Dave said: 'I thought it was going to be our year, but it wasn't to be. We lost 4-3 in the semis to Bolton Wanderers who went on to meet Blackpool in what become known as the Stanley Matthews Final. Much of that semi-final remains a blur to me. I got knocked out early in the game and was concussed, but we staged a magnificent fight back after being 4-0 down and so very nearly turned things our way.'

Evertonians recall that clash as one of the most dramatic in the history of the competition.

Hickson was hurt as early as the 15th minute following a collision with Hartle. By then Bolton had already taken the lead through Holden. Moir added a second before a reluctant Hickson was led off after 25 minutes. By the time he returned to the fray a quarter of an hour later, Wanderers were 3-0 up thanks to Lofthouse, and when the same player made it four in the closing stages of a totally one-sided first half, the Evertonians in the crowd were beginning to think about a cricket score.

Their dismay was heightened when Tommy Clinton missed a penalty on the stroke of half-time, but the second period was football's equivalent to the Charge of the Light Brigade. A John Willie Parker double and a well-taken effort from Farrell had Bolton hanging on like grim death at the final whistle.

Dave said: 'Missing out on Wembley was the biggest disappointment of my career, but the most important thing for the club was to try and gain promotion. We finally got back at the third attempt the following season.'

Hickson and his attacking partner, Parker, claimed the lion's share of the 92 goals which carried Everton back into the First Division in 1953/54. The pair had totally contrasting styles, but they complemented each other perfectly.

Dave was full of running, brave to the point of being reckless and ready to charge headlong into any situation. Defenders either matched him or were trampled under-foot. John Willie was often accused of being lazy, but he

A fierce shot from Dave Hickson hits the side netting in an Everton clash against Preston North End in 1958.

was always in the right place at the right time to accept the many chances created by his willing team-mate.

Parker hit 31 goals, Hickson 25, as Everton stormed back to their rightful place in the top flight. Promotion became a reality against Birmingham City on April 24, 1954. The goal hero, not surprisingly, was Hickson.

A crowd approaching 70,000 packed Goodison, raising the roof after 38 minutes. Famous keeper Gil Merrick double-fisted the ball away, only to see it come flying back with the speed of a bullet from Hickson's head.

If Everton could win 6-0 at Oldham in their final game of the season, they would go up as Champions. By now, the fans were beginning to believe in miracles. The players, supremely confident, set their stall out to achieve the impossible and Oldham prepared for a royal blue invasion.

It was to be a truly remarkable night. The final score was Oldham 0, Everton 4. John Willie bagged two, Hickson and Tommy Jones also hitting the target. Dave said: 'It was asking a lot to go out and score six while keeping a clean sheet, but we really went for it to try and claim top spot. It was a great night, the climax to two tremendous seasons in which we reached the semi-finals of the F.A. Cup and returned to the First Division.

'On the night we gained promotion, I said that the club would never go down again. That's been proved right and I'm proud of everything they've achieved since.'

Dave had reached the peak of his Everton career. The crowd loved him, but his robust style got him into trouble with officials on more than one occasion. He said: 'It was mainly for dissent. I was a winner. I played for the fans and for the club. I was sent off three times, but only once for a tackle. That was during my time with Liverpool and we were 3-0 up at the time! It was just a retaliatory thing that happened in the heat of the moment.'

Because of his style and up-front approach, defenders would try to provoke Dave — for obvious reasons. He never ducked a challenge, saying: 'It was just enthusiasm. I probably loved the game too much. I hated to lose and I think the fans understood that.'

Everton sold Hickson to Aston Villa for £20,000 in November, 1955. He then moved on to Huddersfield Town who were managed at that time by Bill Shankly. Blues fans were thrilled when the bustling centre-forward returned to Goodison Park for £6,500 in July, 1957. He had only been away 18 months and in that time Everton made a handsome £13,000 profit on his transfer — a considerable sum in those days.

Dave immediately reclaimed the number nine shirt that had been worn in his absence by Jimmy Harris, George Kirby and young Derek Temple. Dave was in the driving seat for two seasons, but the 1959/60 campaign was to prove one of the most controversial in the history of Everton F.C.

The Cannonball Kid. Dave Hickson makes a superb flying header against Aston Villa in the 1953 F.A. Cup quarter final.

Hickson was still putting his heart and soul into every game, but in the opening two months of the season he found himself dropped three times despite a return of six goals in a dozen outings. Everton had signed Alan Shackleton from Leeds United and certain members of the board felt Hickson was now expendable.

Arch-rivals Liverpool put in an audacious bid for the man their fans had always looked on as public enemy number one and all hell let loose on Merseyside with emotions running high on both sides of Stanley Park.

The *Liverpool Echo* reported: 'Never in the history of football in this city has there been such a rumpus about a player from one club joining neighbours and rivals. Everton fans have written that if Hickson goes, they will go with him. Liverpool have received warning that if Hickson arrives, some of their most loyal fans will depart! It remains to be seen if these factions will be as good as their word.'

Letters flooded into the paper. One reader lamented: 'Any player capable of scoring 28 goals in 40 odd games, supplied by the type of player whom the board and manager think is suitable, should have a statue erected in his honour.'

Another wrote: 'I have been a loyal supporter since 1945. We have not had much to cheer about since then, except Dave Hickson. Here is a man who has won our admiration because he is so obviously an Evertonian. If Dave goes, so will a lot of the fans.'

Despite the obvious discontent amongst thousands of their fans, Everton went ahead with the deal. Liverpool got their man for £12,000 and so on November 7, 1959, the unthinkable happened.

Hickson, the man who had been Goodison's leading scorer the previous season, pulled on a red number nine shirt and ran out for Liverpool at Anfield in front of 50,000 people.

Aston Villa, one of his former clubs, provided the opposition and, playing alongside a young man by the name of Roger Hunt, the Cannonball Kid proved that it's not so much the colour of the jersey that matters, as the qualities of the man wearing it.

Like a real-life Roy of the Rovers, Hickson scored with a left-foot drive and a spectacular diving header to inspire a 2-0 victory and bring the house down. It must have been strange for him to hear rapturous applause coming from the Kop.

On the same day, Everton crashed 8-2 at Newcastle, but Dave took no satisfaction from his old side's Geordie mauling. He was no longer an Everton player, but he still had tremendous respect for the fans who had saluted his dash and daring on so many occasions.

One of those supporters was Bill Kenwright, later to make a name for himself in his own right as Gordon Clegg in Coronation Street, and, more recently, as the producer

King of the air. Dave Hickson rises above a defender to bullet in a header.

and driving force behind such theatrical hits as *Blood Brothers* and *Joseph and his Amazing Technicolor Dream Coat*. He said: 'You only have one real hero in this life. Dave Hickson was mine. I remember when I was nine or ten and I actually met him in person. I was speechless. He was god as far as I was concerned.

'He still is. In more recent time he has become like a brother to me.'

A Blood Brother perhaps? It all seems rather appropriate when you recall Davie's battling exploits. His number one fan said: 'Dave was the kind of player who you always felt would die for the team. These days, players turn it on if they get up in the right frame of mind in the morning. Dave could be playing in the reserves in front of 20 people and still produce the goals. When he moved to Anfield, I became a Liverpudlian for 24 hours, although that soon wore off.

'I remain a blue. The Dave Hicksons of this world helped you to dream and believe you could achieve the impossible.'

Dave is still playing football and revelling in it — in his sixtieth year! He plays in as many charity games as possible, turning out for teams like the Wavertree Police, the quaintly named Plessey's Over The Hill Mob and Billy Butler's Radio Merseyside XI.

If you are out and about on the Wirral and see a familiar figure jogging along with that unmistakable mop of hair blowing in the wind . . . yes, it's Dave Hickson — training for his next football challenge.

Bring on the tin helmets!

CHAPTER FOUR

Brian Labone

The last of the great Corinthians . . . that was the way the late Harry Catterick described Brian Labone.

It was the ultimate tribute from a great manager to a great centre-half whose Goodison Park career spanned a magnificent 14 years. Incredibly, 'Labby' was only booked twice in 530 fiercely competitive games, playing against some of the roughest and toughest strikers in the business. He was very much the thinking-man's footballer, a giant number five who was cultured rather than cut-throat. He could read the game superbly, giving Everton the kind of long-term stability that money can't buy.

Former chairman Sir John Moores once said of him: 'When you think of loyalty, you think of Labone.'

If you want to get ahead, get a hat . . . preferably the lid of the F.A. Cup. Brian Labone with British football's most famous trophy in 1966.

B

He was a tower of strength when the League Championship came to Goodison in 1963. He was the proudest man in Britain three years later when he became the first Everton skipper since the legendary Dixie Dean to hold aloft the F.A. Cup. When the Championship returned to Goodison in 1970, Labone was still there — captain and kingpin of another great side.

He was one of the old school who survived a football revolution. During his long and distinguished career the game changed beyond recognition.

The maximum wage was scrapped and overnight, it seemed, a sport became big business. Tactics were also revolutionised, the pressures for success becoming that much more acute.

Through it all, Labone remained the model professional, whether he was playing for Everton or England. Little wonder Catterick saluted him as a great Corinthian, a tag that should not be misconstrued.

You don't come through 500 plus matches in the toughest League in the world without being able to take care of yourself. Brian smiles and says: 'I hurt a few, don't you worry about that.'

'Labby' is in insurance these days, which seems rather appropriate. Sound, solid and dependable — he first came to prominence in August, 1957, just a month after leaving the Liverpool Collegiate. The *Liverpool Echo* reported: 'Not so long ago, 17 years old Brian Labone was swotting over his school books and pondering whether to go on to a University education or become a professional footballer.

'Football won. He signed for Everton — to the disappointment of Liverpool — and tomorrow has the task of marking Dave Hickson in a Goodison Park practice match.'

These pre-season games drew very big crowds in the Fifties when foreign tours were virtually non-existent. Labone against Hickson — the grammar school boy against the man who used to eat centre-halves for breakfast. It was a confrontation that captured the imagination of the fans.

Wembley-bound in 1966 . . . former Everton chairman John Moores wishes Brian Labone all the best at Lime Street Station.

Would the 'kid' be trampled underfoot? Certainly, the robust Hickson was keen to make an impression, having re-signed for the Blues after short spells with Villa and Huddersfield. Labone came through his baptism of fire with honours, leap-frogging the junior teams to gain an immediate place in the Reserves.

He said: 'To go straight in at that level from the Mersey-side Grammar Schools side was a little bit like climbing the Matterhorn. I avoided the A, B and C teams in which many youngsters get lost in the scramble to get on. I was in the public eye from the word go, which was daunting in one respect.

'In those days, you were automatically promoted to the first team if the man in your position was injured.

'There was no squad system in which experienced people would be shuffled around in an emergency. I would watch Tommy T.E. Jones and turn white every time he went down.'

Equally, Brian would tingle with excitement at the prospect of pulling on a first-team shirt for the team he had idolised from the terraces as a lad. He didn't have to wait long for his big chance. Jones had a recurrence of a groin injury before a game at Birmingham City on March 29, 1958 and 18 years old Labone was in at the deep end.

The Everton team that day was Dunlop, Sanders, Tansey, Rea, Labone, Meagan, J. Harris, Temple, Hickson, Fielding and Williams. No such thing as substitutes, of course.

It's interesting to compare that side with the line-up in Brian's last game in an Everton shirt, 13 years later on August 24, 1971. In football terms, the Blues had moved on at least four generations, the fans roaring on West, Scott, K. Newton, Kendall, Labone, Harvey, Husband, Ball, Johnson, Hurst, Morrissey and young substitute Mike Lyons who took Brian's shirt in the following game before handing it over to Everton's next number five, Roger Kenyon.

It's impossible to relate those two teams in any way, shape or form. When young Labone took centre stage in 1958, he couldn't have imagined — even in his wildest dreams — that his career would take in the Fifties, Sixties and the start of the Seventies.

The man was a veritable pillar of Everton and, to this day, only Ted Sagar has amassed more League appearances, Labby finishing up just 12 games short of the immortal keeper's all-time record.

That debut at Birmingham ended in defeat. Brian stepped down, but was recalled within two weeks for a testing home debut against Tottenham. A Hickson double couldn't prevent the Londoners from snatching a 4-3

Action man . . . Brian Labone in the thick of the action, with twin centre-back John Hurst playing a supporting role.

triumph, and with typical honesty Brian recalls: 'I think I was at fault for at least three of their goals, but the fans were tremendous. I was up against Bobby Smith and it made me realise what a hard and punishing game it was, especially for a centre-half.

'If you were half a yard short or a split second late with a challenge, the ball would end up in the back of the net. I went back into the Reserves and started to learn, making just four appearances the following season. After that I was in, virtually all the way through.'

Brian was soon coming to terms with some of the game's wiliest centre-forwards, men like Andy Lockhead who was known as the Burnley assassin. Brian said: 'We had another name for him — Andy Blockhead! He would try to break your leg and then shake you by the hand. There were lots of tremendous number nines in those early days, men like Wyn Davies and Ron Davies, Bronco Lane and David Herd.

'As time went on, strikers became much more subtle. The old 2-3-5 formation was replaced by 4-2-4. The long ball down the middle was not quite so prevalent. Teams had to operate with twin centre-backs, which is when John Hurst joined me at the heart of the Blues' defence.

'The game became much harder and made you think a lot more, simply because centre-forwards were becoming much more mobile. It was no longer a case of the five marking the nine, the traditional battle. Forwards would try to pull you out of position and so you stopped marking numbers and had to concentrate that little bit harder.'

The 1962 and 1966 World Cups had inspired coaches to think long and hard about a game which had been stereotyped for years. It was in the aftermath of the '62 competition in Chile that Brian gained his first England cap, playing in October against Northern Ireland in Belfast. It was quite an achievement because he was the first Everton player since the war to be capped at senior level by England. He was 22 and it was to be the first of 26 international appearances.

Brian Labone and rival skipper Don Megson shakes hands before the 1966 F.A. Cup Final between Everton and Sheffield Wednesday.

It was to be a memorable season for Labone who missed only two games as the Blues swept to the Championship. By now the big defender was playing under his third Everton manager. He had been signed by Ian Buchan, a coach who was something of a fitness fanatic. Buchan was a former Loughborough College man and a physical training expert: 'He had us running round like headless chickens,' said Brian.

The next boss, Johnny Carey, probably went to the other extreme. Many feel Carey was unlucky to lose his job in 1961, having signed some outstanding players. His successor Harry Catterick was tough, uncompromising, but highly successful, reaping the benefit of some of Carey's acquisitions.

Equally, he signed some fine players himself, men like goalkeeper Gordon West, half-back Tony Kay whose career was later wrecked by a bribes scandal stemming from his days with Sheffield Wednesday, and flying winger Alex Scott.

It didn't take long for the players to find out just how tough Harry could be. Brian said: 'We went on a summer trip to New York, staying in the Paramount Hotel on West 46th Street just off Broadway. We had only been there 24 hours when I saw Roy Vernon, the club captain and one of our best players, heading out of the door carrying his suitcase. He had contravened the curfew and was on his way home!'

Catterick became the man many players loved to hate, but Labone said: 'When he first came, he was very straight and fair with me. Many of the papers were saying "Labone is promising, but it's a tender age to hold the Everton defence together". He stuck with me and we began to build an excellent side.

'Vernon and Alex Young began to put the goals away. Vernon was a great inside forward, but he was the most unlikely playing specimen you've ever seen. He didn't have a pick on him, but he would always guarantee you a goal or two inside 20 minutes. Roy was a straight talker who would give you a rollicking if he felt it was needed, but it was all for the good of the team. He was a tremendous penalty taker and had a hell of a shot, mainly all right foot, but with a short back lift and a lot of power.

'Then there was my great mate, Gordon West, my room mate and a brilliant goalkeeper who was also one of the funniest people you could wish to meet. I can remember playing at Newcastle in October, 1967. It was 0-0 and the game was nearly over when West flattened striker Bennett. The ref gave a penalty and sent Gordon off.

'Sandy Brown had come on earlier as a substitute and as he was our man for all positions, he suddenly found himself in goal. His first touch was to try to save this penalty which he duly failed to do.

Buddies on and off the field . . . Brian Labone and that famous Everton 'keeper Gordon West.

'No one could blame Sandy for the defeat, but Westy spent the entire journey home giving him down the banks for diving the wrong way — and making a good case of it as well!'

In the wake of the 1963 title triumph, manager Catterick started to look ahead. Ray Wilson would eventually arrive with a superb tactical brain and a cultured left foot to take over the left-back berth that had been occupied in the main by Mick Meagan. A young Colin Harvey would bring skill, work rate and superb positional play to the midfield and another local boy, Tommy Wright, would take over at right-back from that classic defender Alex Parker.

The F.A. cup, soccer's holy grail, was the next target and it was very much in Everton's sights in 1966. By now, Labone was ranked closely behind Leeds United star Jack Charlton in the England rankings. Everyone on Merseyside believed the Everton man had a great chance with the World Cup looming on home soil in the summer, but the big defender made a shock request to be overlooked so that he could go ahead with his planned summer marriage to former Miss Liverpool, Pat Lynam.

That news was soon overshadowed when Labone fulfilled a boyhood dream by leading Everton to victory at Wembley in the Cup. It remains one of the greatest fightbacks in the history of the competition. Two down, the Blues stormed back thanks to a double from the most unlikely hero on the field, Mike Trebilcock, and a sensational Derek Temple winner.

Brian said: 'Many of the game's greatest players never get the chance to hold aloft the F.A. Cup so that was a very special moment for me.'

Brian had the Cup medal he had always dreamed about. He had a Championship medal as well, and to all extents and purposes, the world was his oyster.

But the Everton captain was beginning to feel the pressure that goes hand in hand with life at the very top, not least in a city where football is everything. Sixteen months after that Wembley final, on September 21, 1967, Labone dropped a bombshell when he announced his retirement.

The 28 year old defender revealed that he was not enjoying his football and that he would be quitting the game he had served so well at the end of his contract or earlier if Everton could find a suitable replacement. He had no intentions of leaving the club without experienced cover, a point boss Catterick touched on when he responded to the announcement.

'It's typical of Brian's top-class character,' said Catterick, 'that he has told me 18 months before the end of his contract that he is going to leave the game. Many a player

Back on his old hunting ground . . . Brian Labone in reflective mood at Goodison Park in 1973.

would not have told his club until the last possible minute. Brian is one of the greatest club men I have ever known. I can understand his mind over this decision and we shall be very sorry to see him go.'

Looking back, Brian said: 'My father had a central heating business and he had always been keen for me to go into that. Equally, I wasn't playing particularly well. You tend to take more of the responsibility when you're a local lad playing for your home town team. Football was weighing heavy on my shoulders at that moment in time.'

The announcement had a profound effect on Brian. Having got it out into the open, he suddenly began to play some of the best football of his career. Just two months later he was recalled to the England squad when Jack Charlton pulled out with a neck injury. His confidence began to soar and he said: 'It was a little lesson in life. When you face up to the inevitable, you relax a bit.'

Eye on the ball and another victory . . . Brian Labone in action against Preston North End in 1976.

The conjecture about his departure continued for a full 16 months, but Everton and England were delighted when, on January 7, 1969, Brian announced that he would be staying on. His father played a part in his decision, as did the fans and manager Harry Catterick. Labone would battle on, using his experience and ability to the full to bolster the youngsters in a very ambitious team.

The man who had led a Football League XI against the Irish two months earlier and once captained an F.A. Select side in Canada, would now strike for glory again with his club and country. He was a key figure when the Championship returned to Goodison in 1970, a season in which he chalked up his 500th first-team appearance when he turned out against Southampton on January 17th.

Brian injured his back in March and subsequently missed the title run-in, but he had played his part. The Mexico World Cup beckoned him in the summer and he played in what was one of the best England sides for a long time.

The last of the Corinthians played his final game for the Blues in the 1971/72 campaign. He had served the club he idolised with total dedication, famous chairman John Moores saying: 'I rejoiced in his play for Everton and England. What an example he has been to everyone. We're proud of Labone.'

The legendary Dixie Dean paid Brian the ultimate compliment during the champagne launch of the centre-half's well-deserved testimonal fund. He said: 'I saw Brian throughout his career. Nobody can ever forget T.G. Jones when talking of the great centre halves, but I rate Labone on a par with him.'

At the end of the *Official History of Everton* video, fans revel in a little bit of Brian Labone theatre. The great FA Cup Final and Championship skipper looks straight into the camera and says: 'One Evertonian is worth 20 Liverpudlians!'

Labby always had a way with words. Once a blue, always a blue.

FULL INTERNATIONAL CAPS
(England score given first in each case)

1963: Northern Ireland 3-1, Wales 4-0, France 2-5.
1967: Spain 2-0, Austria 1-0.
1968: Scotland 1-1, Spain 2-1, Sweden 3-1, Yugoslavia 0-1, Russia 2-0, West Germany 0-1.
1969: Northern Ireland 3-1, Scotland 4-1, Rumania 0-0, Bulgaria 1-1, Mexico 0-0, Uruguay 2-1, Brazil 1-2.
1970: Scotland 0-0, Wales 1-1, Belgium 3-1, Columbia 4-0, Ecuador 2-0, Rumania 1-0, Brazil 0-1, West Germany 2-3.
Total: 26.

CHAPTER FIVE

Alex Young

Alex Young was more than an Everton player. He was a Goodison God.

The fair-haired Scot inspired such adulation during his eight years on Merseyside that his place in this book was never open to debate. The fans who revelled in their football in Liverpool during the Swinging Sixties will never forget the will-o'-the-wisp centre-forward whose auto-biography could so easily have been called *Tales of the Unexpected.*

Master of the unorthodox, a genius in football boots, Young was every inch the 'Golden Vision' to the Evertonians who worshipped him as a fully paid-up member of the School of Soccer Science.

Signed from Hearts on November 23rd, 1960 in a £55,000 deal that also brought full-back George Thomson to Goodison, Young was soon to win over the fans with his guile and class. He arrived with a sound pedigree, having already played six times for Scotland's senior side as well as winning Scottish League and Cup winners medals with Hearts.

The supporters at Tynecastle were bitterly disappointed to see Alex go. He had signed for the Edinburgh outfit as an 18-year-old from Newtongrange Star and in five seasons scored 77 goals, including 20 in the club's record-breaking 1957/58 Championship campaign and 23 when they recaptured the title in 1959/60.

Little wonder a posse of English clubs had been tracking the player. Manchester United, Chelsea, West Brom and Wolves all asked Hearts to keep them informed about any developments, but it was Everton and Preston who backed up their interest with identical cash bids of £40,000. An

Defenders usually found themselves trailing in the wake of Everton's 'Golden Vision', Alex Young.

intriguing battle of wits developed between rival bosses Johnny Carey of Everton and North End's Cliff Britton, ironically an ex-Goodison player!

Both managers travelled north of the border on the same day, hoping to persuade Young to sign. Carey and Britton actually boarded the same train and they even lunched together en route. The conversation must have been rather interesting.

Carey, working closely with influential and ambitious chairman John Moores, was determined to re-establish the Blues as a First Division force. He was particularly keen to sign a class centre-forward and there were reports that Everton had made offers for Hibernian's Joe Baker (later to make a name for himself in Italy) and a certain Brian Clough, Middlesbrough's free-scoring front man.

When the news broke that Hearts were ready to talk money for Young, Carey wasted little time in tabling his bid. Preston appeared to be favourites at first, but indecision at board level cost them a football genius. Alex recalls: 'To be honest, I was going to sign for Preston because they offered me a bigger signing-on fee. I'd more or less put pen to paper with Mr Britton very keen to go through with the deal. But one or two of his directors baulked, even though the signing-on fees then were not very big.

'They wouldn't back him straight away and, being the man he was, he tore up the forms.'

Carey stepped in and Young linked up with Bobby Collins, Jimmy Gabriel, Alex Parker and Hearts team mate Thomson to form a powerful Anglo-Scottish contingent at Goodison.

Alex arrived on Merseyside carrying a nasty knee injury sustained playing for the British Army in a 'friendly' against Aberdeen at Pittodrie. The blond striker must have looked a picture arriving at Goodison for the first time with a backsplint on his leg.

He was subsequently unavailable for three weeks, but that only heightened the fans' expectations. When he

Alex Young, head and shoulders above his rivals as usual. In action here against Ipswich Town.

finally made his debut, against Spurs on December 17, 1960, the *Liverpool Echo* set the scene by reporting: 'Young is a thoroughbred, a great mover with the ball, fast, active and razor sharp in his reactions. For his size, he is a good header of the ball. He is clever, artistic and can score goals.'

Given that kind of build-up, the man himself was desperate to produce the goods, especially as his debut was at Goodison. But he still hadn't completely recovered from the knee problem, lacking the sharpness that was vital to his game. Everton lost 3-1 and no one was more disappointed than Alex.

He said: 'I played alongside Frank Wignall in that game. Carey put me in, but I wasn't really ready to play. I still had a lot of muscle wastage on my injured left leg. Spurs were a superb team at that time and they beat us fairly convincingly on the day.'

Alex stepped down for four matches after that ill-fated debut. Everton's form was very inconsistent at that time and in a disastrous spell they lost 3-0 to Burnley, 4-1 to both Leicester and Wolves, 2-1 to Bolton and 4-0 to West Ham. The fans took heart from the blossoming partnership of Young and Welsh international inside-forward Roy Vernon.

When the Scot plundered his first goals for the Blues, a double against Blackburn Rovers at the end of March, it was the signal for a storming finish to the season. Everton won six of their remaining seven games, thrashing the likes of Newcastle, Cardiff and Arsenal. The Goodison outfit finished fifth, but it was not good enough to save Carey, the manager whose astute swoops in the transfer market had led to the capture of men like Vernon, Billy Bingham, Jimmy Gabriel — and Young.

These players would spark Everton's push towards the game's top honours, but under a new boss . . . Harry Catterick. Powerful chairman Moores sacked Carey during a taxi ride from a Football League meeting in London. To this day, whenever a manger is under serious pressure, you'll hear Evertonians talking about the possibility of him 'taking a taxi' — in other words, getting the bullet.

Alex had an interesting theory about the Carey affair. He said: 'It was quite sad. We were just picking up nicely when he lost the job. If I had been properly fit when he signed me, I don't think Carey would have lost his job. I had been in tremendous form for Hearts and if I'd been able to reproduce that straight away with Everton, I don't think we would have lost too many games. In a way, Johnny Carey paid heavily for my injury.

'It was a traumatic time for all the lads, not least for me. I never saw eye to eye with Harry Catterick. I know he was one of the most successful managers Everton have ever had, but he wasn't my type of boss.'

Alex Young signs on for Everton in 1960, watched by chairman John Moores, manager Johnny Carey and George Thomson who arrived in a joint deal from Hearts.

If the players had their reservations, for whatever reasons, John Moores was convinced Catterick was the man for the job. The chairman was not a man to trifle with. Catterick decided to take the team to the United States in the summer, keen to assess the strengths and weaknesses of every member of his squad. Young was still very much an Army man and red tape was threatening to keep him at home.

Moores stepped in, approaching Mr Reginald Bevin, the Postmaster General and M.P. for the Liverpool constituency of Toxteth.

He took up the matter personally with Mr John Profumo, the Secretary for War who was later to make more headlines than a hundred football teams when the London call girl scandal unfolded involving Christine Keeler. Mr Profumo was one of the most powerful men in the country. I don't know if Mr Bevin told him that the Army couldn't mess around with the 'Golden Ghost' as Young was already being dubbed (the famous Golden Vision tag would come later). Whatever the case, the talented forward was granted leave of absence and Catterick was able to prepare smoothly for his first full season at the helm.

Alex scored on the opening day of the 61/62 campaign, playing his part in a 2-0 home victory over Aston Villa. Incredibly, Everton lost five of their next six matches, but Catterick was a shrewd and single-minded boss who would soon find that elusive winning formula.

Everton eventually finished fourth, one place better than the previous season wrapping up an eventful season with an astonishing 8-3 home win over struggling Cardiff and a 3-2 triumph at Arsenal where Young bagged two typical goals. The Scot had figured in 40 of the 42 League games, an appearance record bettered only by rock-solid half-back Gabriel and centre-half Brian Labone.

The following season, he would be one of only two ever-presents as the famous Championship trophy returned to Goodison for the first time since 1939. Young scored in each of the opening three games, all victories. He would plunder 22 League goals by the end of the season and captivate the Goodison fans with his artistry. His lone-goal winner at home to Tottenham on April 20, 1963 took Everton to the top of the table and they were never going to be dislodged.

When Fulham arrived on Merseyside on May 11, it was all about a title tango. Young's partner in goals, Roy Vernon, netted a hat-trick, Alex 'Chico' Scott was also on the scoresheet, and Goodison erupted.

The Championship side was full of skill, power and aggression — the perfect blend. Alex and skipper Vernon scored 46 goals between them, mesmerising defences the length and breadth of the country. Alex said: 'We used to rely on skill, throwing lots of dummies to fool defenders.

Great pals and great players . . . Alex Young and Everton team mate Alan Ball enjoy a day at the races.

It's a tactic you don't see these days. Forwards are happy to lay the ball back.

'Tony Kay arrived on the scene and he was some player, a real powerhouse with ability to match. He could sit on the ball and play and also bully opponents off the ball with his aggression. We had two outstanding ball winners in Kay and Jimmy Gabriel.'

Alex will never forget that May day when Everton beat Fulham 4-1 and claimed the title. He said: 'The crowd were tremendous, as usual. Rival players often froze against us because of the atmosphere generated by our fans. I've still got very strong feelings for the place. I love Merseyside.

'A lot of cities leave you feeling cold, but I felt a special affinity with Liverpool. I was proud to play with so many great players in front of those terrific Everton supporters.'

Like most players with flair and genius, Young was an enigma. He set himself incredibly high standards and on those occasions when he failed to hit the heights, he was hyper-critical of his own game. It was a point he dealt with in some detail at the start of the 1967/68 season which was to be his last in an Everton shirt.

By now, he had added an F.A. Cup winners medal to his trophy haul, playing his part in that great Wembley fight back against Sheffield Wednesday in 1966. But despite all of his success, he was beginning to ask questions about his own game, almost as if he needed reassurance from the fans who still worshipped the very ground he walked on.

He went on record as saying: 'There have been times when I have had out-of-this-world games, matches in which everything I've attempted has turned to gold, duels in which, with a minimum of effort, I've run rings round floundering defenders and laid on goals for my colleagues in the Everton attack.

'Yet there have been times when I've exasperated myself and must have stretched the patience of manager Harry Catterick.'

Searching for an answer, Young reflected on his days at Hearts where a trainer by the name of Johnny Harvey had that very special knack of bringing out the best in all the men under his charge. Harvey could read Alex like a book and knew he needed more than a kick up the backside to produce the goods. Here was a player who thrived on an inspirational pep talk — and Harvey was always the man to provide it.

Alex said: 'All Johnny did was pump into me how good I was. I would step out for Hearts feeling ten feet tall. I never had anybody doing that for me at Goodison — except the fans. All through my career with Everton there was no one

Members of the airborne ballet? Schofield, the Birmingham goal-keeper, leaps to claim a centre from Alex Young in a clash at Goodison in 1963.

behind the scenes who tried to lift me like that. Amazingly enough, the only time I was inspired off the park at Goodison was in a benefit game for Dixie Dean.

'The Scots of Everton and Liverpool combined to play the English players at the two clubs. My manager was the great Bill Shankly. He made me feel great before the game. I was the type of player who needed something like that. I certainly never got it in our dressing room from Harry Catterick or any of the coaches!

'I drew my inspiration from the crowd. Catterick wasn't a tracksuit manager. He was very distant from the players. Shankly would always praise his own team and he was prepared to have a go at the opposition when it was called for. I always felt that Catterick praised up the opposition. It might have been to get our backs up, but it certainly didn't do anything for me.'

It sounds stange now to hear the Golden Vision, arch

enemy number one to the Liverpudlians of the day, talking in glowing terms about the manager across the park, but his words are genuine. He said: 'I really admired Shankly. I think lots of Evertonians did without saying it at the time. It was a great experience having him in the dressing room before that Dean game.

'Everyone was in a great mood. He was coaxing us to go out and produce the goods and, as I said, I wasn't used to that type of encouragement in the Everton dressing room.'

Clearly, Young craved a Shankly — or a Johnny Harvey — in his corner. Catterick was a very different kind of motivator. He was distant from the players, a ruthless disciplinarian who must have appeared cold and calculating to the men he drove on relentlessly from one game to the next. Young didn't play for the manager.

He performed for the supporters on the terraces whose loyalty, on one occasion, went above and beyond the call of duty. A better expression might be 'over the top'.

When Catterick dropped Young for a game at Blackpool during Everton's 1966 Cup Final season — choosing to give a debut to a 16 years old budding star by the name of Joe Royle — it was reported that a group of fans physically attacked the manager in a car park confrontation that made headline news. It was a disgraceful assault, but it summed up the depth of feeling the supporters had for Young.

The irony is that young Royle eventually became an Everton giant in his own right. But back in 1966, Alex was the 'king'. The Scot is also convinced that the Blackpool incident was over-played, for whatever reason, by Catterick. Alex was with the Reserves at Goodison when the 'attack' was unfolding at Bloomfield Road, but was told by a group of senior players that the affair was blown up out of all proportion.

Equally, he will never forget his manager's reaction when it came to selecting a team the following week for the game at Northampton. Catterick brought back Young and also included Jimmy Gabriel in the side, saying he was picking the 'hooligans' team'.

Alex said: 'For several games after that, Catterick never came into the dressing room before matches. He took the reins again in that respect when it looked as if his hooligans' team might win the Cup which we duly did.'

For their part, the fans were unaware of the friction between manager and superstar, which is what Young was at that time. On Wednesday, April 13, 1968, the *Liverpool Echo's* television page declared: 'Tonight is Everton night, so Blue you might almost think you have colour television. The Golden Vision will unfold on your screens.

'Written by Neville Smith in partnership with ITN newscaster Gordon Honeycombe, the BBC 1 production covers a week in the life of Everton FC, its players and fans. The Golden Vision is Alex Young and the play centres on the men whose chief obsession is football in general and Everton in particular.

'They eat, sleep and drink football and their wives and girlfriends are inexorably involved in the endless soccer discussions and preparations for Saturday.'

Incredibly, the Golden Vision's Everton career was almost at an end. In August, at the age of 31, Alex Young became player-manager of Glentoran. He spent just two months across the Irish Sea, returning to join Stockport County. He was forced to retire with knee trouble in August, 1969.

In any case, Stockport's Edgeley Park ground was no place for an aristocrat like Young. I think of him only as an Everton player, a cutting in the *Liverpool Echo* library summing up his qualities perfectly . . .

'Young was one of the classiest players in post-war football. Not for him the storm-tossed battles of brawn and ill-will. He brought a fluency, grace and charm to football, but for all that he possessed a vicious shot and a heading ability way above average.

His fans idolised him and his name apeared on gable ends throughout Merseyside — always followed by the words . . . THE GREATEST!'

FULL INTERNATIONAL CAPS
(Scotland score given first in each case)

1960: England 1-1, Austria (sub) 1-4, Hungary 3-3, Turkey 2-4.
1961: Wales 0-2, Northern Ireland 5-2, Portugal 0-1, Eire 3-0.
Total: 8.

CHAPTER SIX

Colin Harvey

Colin Harvey was the original marathon man.

Watching him working like a trojan from penalty area to penalty area was an inspirational sight. Quite simply, Harvey was the ultimate midfield player.

A banner used to be hoisted high at Goodison Park declaring him the 'White Pele'. To an outsider, the sentiment might seem over the top.

To the supporters who revelled in his all-action play, it was an ideal way of expressing the utmost respect for a man whose skill and dedication helped to light up in Goodison in the Sixties and early Seventies.

Harvey made a sensational entrance into top-class football when he was thrown into a European Cup clash against Italian giants Inter Milan in the white-hot atmosphere of the intimidating San Siro Stadium in 1963.

He survived this baptism of fire to develop into a classical performer who had all the attributes to shine at the very highest level.

Ironically, he won just one England cap, against Malta in February, 1971. The only way the Evertonians could explain it away was to say that their idol was 'too artistic' for Sir Alf Ramsey, who might have reaped a rich reward if he had chosen to transfer the famous Ball-Harvey-Kendall midfield triangle onto an international stage.

The trio, as well as being almost telepathic, possessed all the qualities needed to tackle world-class opposition. I don't know if it ever crossed Ramsey's mind to play them together, particularly during that golden spell around 1969/70.

If it did, he chose to ignore his instincts. For while Ball won 72 caps for his country, the dynamic duo who played alongside him for the Blues were consistently overlooked — a fact that bamboozled Merseyside's knowledgeable football fraternity.

People use the phrase 'a self-made man'. Terry Darracott believes Harvey was 'a self-made player'.

He explained: 'Colin was a very dedicated, hard-working individual who got to the top because he was prepared to do that little bit extra. I always remember when I was an apprentice and he was 19 or 20 and becoming a regular in the first team. He would always put in that extra half-hour after training, no matter what he had done in the morning.

'At the same time, Colin always had time for the younger boys and I always admired him for that. It costs nothing to go over to a kid and say 'Hey, I noticed you doing something this morning. I didn't think it was quite right.' Or, if a lad had done something good, to say to him 'Well done, I thought that was smashing.'

'I can only recall my day as a young player. If one of the senior pros ever spoke to me, I would float all the way home. Colin was that type and it went towards making him a great footballer.'

Harvey was brought up in Fazakerley in the north end of Liverpool. An Evertonian from the word go thanks to his father and grandfather, he attended Holy Name School where he was soon showing his potential on the football field. A cup and league double was won, but when young Harvey was 'transferred' to Cardinal Allen High School, a mini-panic set in.

It was a rugby stronghold, but Colin was relieved to learn that his year — the boys who had come through the 13-plus examination — were allowed to play soccer.

Even then, the fixture list was only quite small, featuring games against local rivals such as Quarry Bank and De La Salle. Whisper it quietly, but the great Evertonian actually had a trial with Liverpool.

Colin recalls: 'I went to a session at the Melwood Training Ground one Tuesday night. Ian Callaghan (later to play over 800 times for the Reds) was a part-time

Down . . . but soon on the up and up in Everton's 1970 Championship season. All action-midfielder Colin Harvey.

professional and he played in the match. Ian was head and shoulders above everyone else and I thought to myself 'That's the standard you must attain.'

'They told me to come back the following week, but in the meantime, I was invited for a trial at Goodison. The training used to take place where the car park is now behind the Stanley Park End. After that, there was no way I was going back to Liverpool.'

Colin played a few 'C' team games before the season was out. He trained the following summer at Bellefield under the watchful eye of Les Shannon and was delighted when it over lapped with the first team's pre-season training. Over a six-week period, his fitness and strength improved considerably and he was revelling in the work.

But he had left school and was beginning to think about his future. He went for an interview with the D.H.S.S. in Upper Parliament Street and was told they had a vacancy as a Filing Clerk. Colin accepted and was told to start on the Monday.

On the Saturday he played for Everton's 'B' team and Les Shannon asked him about training on the Monday. When Colin revealed he was working, the startled coach said: 'What have you done that for? Chief Scout Harry Cook wants to talk to you.'

Cook turned up at Harvey's house on the Monday evening and asked if Colin wanted to sign professional terms. Thus ended the shortest working career in the history of the Department of Health and Social Security.

Colin said: 'I had to go in the next day and tell them I was packing in. They pointed out that they would have given me two weeks' notice and so I had to do the same! I agreed to work out my time and, at the end of it, they all had a whip-round to buy me a few leaving presents. It could only happen in Liverpool.'

It was 1961 and Harvey was 16. He enjoyed the discipline and training that was part and parcel of a soccer apprentice's life. Everton were beginning to get their act together on the first-team front, having had a frustrating time in the Fifties.

In 1963, the Blues won the Championship. Colin, still trying to make the breakthrough, said: 'The team had some fantastic characters and they played some great football that year. On the day Everton beat Fulham at Goodison to clinch the title, I was selected for an 'A' team game at Bellefield. We all rushed back to Goodison to see the big match and it was quite an occasion.

'After the summer break, I had a good pre-season and was going well in the reserves. We played at Sheffield and on the way back we stopped off at Belle Vue in Manchester for something to eat. The first team were travelling to Italy

Snowman . . . Colin Harvey gets a gee up from assistant trainer Arthur Proudler at an icy training session in February, 1969.

on the Monday for their big European Cup game against Inter Milan. Gordon Watson phoned through to see if any of the reserves were to travel and about three or four of us were told we were on the trip.'

Colin was convinced he was going along to carry the skips, but on the afternoon of the game, manager Harry Catterick called a meeting and read out the team . . . West, Parker, Meagan, Stevens, Labone, Harris, Scott, HARVEY, Young, Vernon and Temple.

The news was sensational and all eyes focused on the young 18 years old debutant in the volatile San Siro Stadium. Colin said: 'People like Suarez and Jair were famous all over the Continent. I knew all of the Milan names because I've always been a regular reader of the *World Soccer* magazine. They even signed a German who was only eligible for the European games. That's how determined they were to lift the trophy.

'When I stepped out onto the pitch, the atmosphere was incredible. I've never known anything like it, before or since.

'I suppose there was a bit of added glamour because it was my first game, but the feeling of intimidation and hate that was generated by the crowd was unbelievable. It did me no harm and I didn't feel overawed. I was nervous, but that suited me. If I ever felt calm before a game, I was worried. I used to like the adrenalin to be pumping.'

The teams had drawn 0-0 at Goodison and so the return was always going to be tense and very tight. In the final reckoning, a goal from Jair — one of the fastest wingers in the world — settled it.

The *Liverpool Echo* reported: 'Everton came to within an ace of forcing a replay. The gamble of playing Harvey was an enormous one, but it nearly paid off. This young Liverpool boy will look back on his first senior game with some pride since he fought hard, played at time with a veteran coolness and could have been a scorer with either of two overhead flips when standing with his back to goal.'

I once asked Harry Catterick about that Milan game and Harvey's debut. The late Everton manager told me: 'Colin was always going to be a great competitor. He was a quiet fellow, introvert as a player, but with superb skills. He was very quick and had a lot of mobility, the ideal professional in my book. He was the kind of lad who could exercise his skills both defensively and deep in his opponents' territory.'

The marathon man theory, summed up perfectly by the boss who nurtured and then exploited the talent.

A couple of days after that European tie, the Blues were due to meet Liverpool in a mighty derby confrontation. Colin was hoping to keep his place for an equally memorable League debut, but that wasn't to come until much later in the campaign. He managed just two First Division games that season, but established himself in the side in 1964/65 after being called up for a tough outing in mid-September against Manchester United.

The dynamic duo . . . young men who would play a dramatic role in the Everton success story . . . Colin Harvey and Howard Kendall.

That match finished in a 2-1 defeat, but a couple of days later the Blues plundered a 4-0 victory over the arch-enemy from Anfield. Harvey was on the scoresheet, along with Morrisey, Pickering and Temple.

Colin was to get 32 League games under his belt as the Blues finished fourth in the table. The 1965/66 season now loomed and the ever-improving Harvey was now bombing along, inspired by team-mate Jimmy Gabriel. Colin said: 'Gabby's courage had to rub off on you. He was a great influence on me.'

1966 was going to be a memorable football year in every way. England won the World Cup, hard on the heels of Everton producing one of the greatest fightbacks of all time in an F.A. Cup Final.

Looking back, Harvey believes the day was dramatic rather than classic, but the Evertonians in the crowd will never forget the way the Blues shrugged off a 2-0 deficit to come storming back thanks to a Mike Trebilcock double and a magnificent Derek Temple winner.

C

Colin singled out goalkeeper Gordon West, skipper and centre-half Brian Labone and defensive wing-half Brian Harris as three key Wembley figures. He said: 'Labby was just reaching his peak and was solid as a rock in the middle of the defence. Harris had always done a good job for the club. In this match, he started bringing the ball out just when we needed it while Westy's drive and ability inspired us all.

'Gordon used to throw the ball out, rather than kick it after struggling for about four months with a thigh injury. He was a great character, but also a very good keeper. In training he would say 'Right, no one is going to score for the next 30 minutes.'

'He would live by his word and was one of the most athletic keepers around.'

Harvey believes Everton were too rigid in the early stages of the Final, sticking with a 4-2-4 formation, despite the fact that Wednesday deployed three men in midfield. He said: 'Jimmy Gabriel and myself were overrun in the first 30 minutes when they were well on top. We could give little support to our front men at that stage.

'The video of the game suggests that a lot of our players were physically shattered early on.

'It had nothing to do with fitness. It was in the days before the offside trap shortened the game, or rather the area in which players are able to get tackles in. You can squeeze things more now in that tight space either side of the half-way line, but then it was a longer game and you ran a lot more to support your defenders and attackers.

'I remember that it was a steaming hot afternoon. The pitch was more energy-sapping in those days. It was a real bowling green and famous for an injury a season.'

It certainly looked ominous for the Blues when McCalliog and Ford gave Wednesday an emphatic lead. Colin said: 'People who had been outstanding for us seemed to lose some of their edge on the day. We were looking to special players like Alex Young and Alex Scott to pull out that little bit extra, but we struggled to a degree

Everton v West Ham in February, 1967 . . . and Gordon West dives to smother the ball as Hammers inside-forward Bennett closes in, watched by Colin Harvey.

up front. Then Mike Trebilcock produced those two goals to pull us level.

'It meant our tails were up while they were totally deflated and Derek Temple raced forward to score one of the best goals ever in a Final for the winner. It was a very emotional moment and my first reaction when it was all over was 'What a brilliant game'.

'You're still believing it a couple of days later with everyone still talking about the victory, but when you analyse the 90 minutes with a clear mind, you have to admit that perhaps it wasn't such a good match for the neutrals.

'It was certainly dramatic and all the more exciting for me because I had been down at Wembley in two of the three previous years, watching Manchester United beat Leicester and Liverpool beat Leeds.

'I travelled with a few mates for the Reds' Final and the atmosphere that day was unbelievable. As an Evertonian, it made my journey back there the following year wearing a blue shirt all the more satisfying.

'We had the chance to bring the trophy back to Goodison for the first time in 33 years and I looked on that as a tremendous honour. My grandad had told me all about his hero Dixie Dean and the way he had carried the Cup through the streets of Liverpool on the back of a horse-drawn carriage. The fact that my grandad was up in the stands with about 50 close relatives and friends made it an extra special occasion for me.

'We won the Cup against all the odds in the end and in that sense it was a great day for Everton. That's how it should be remembered.'

Colin was proud to have played alongside the likes of Young and Gabriel, contrasting players but both real crowd pleasers. One of the highlights of that Final came near the end when Gabriel played the ball against a corner flag and defied the Wednesday players to come and get it. He finally won a throw-in, thrusting his arms into the air like a Champion boxer who had just knocked out an opponent with a sucker punch.

Yes, 1966 was a vintage year, but manager Catterick would soon be building for the future, Colin reflecting on the arrival of Alan Ball and Howard Kendall and the emergence of such talented young players as Joe Royle, John Hurst and Jimmy Husband.

The next milestone would be that glorious Championship year of 1970. Colin said: 'Every single player in that side was tremendous in his own right. Gordon West was an outstanding keeper and a great shot stopper. Right-back Tommy Wright had begun his career as an inside-forward and so he was quick. He was also a great defensive header of the ball. On the other side, Sandy Brown was strong with either foot, a great striker of the ball.

'He was also the butt of many of Gordon West's jokes which meant there was never a dull moment in the

West Ham keeper Bobby Ferguson dives at the feet of the in-running Colin Harvey at Goodison in 1972.

dressing room. Many people remember Sandy for that incredible own goal he scored against Liverpool at Goodison in 1969. It's often forgotten that he had been one of our match-winners when we beat them 3-1 at Goodison in 1966.

'Brian Labone was the best centre-half of his type at that time. He was consistent, solid in the air and could also use the ball well. Alongside him, John Hurst was a great reader of the game. He also had an eye for an important goal, like Derek Mountfield in more recent times.

'Jimmy Husband on the right wing was a really good mover. On the left, Johnny Morrissey would drop in as a fourth midfield player. He could hold things up, was a good crosser and he was also very strong in the tackle. Johnny didn't get the credit for the work he did. He was always very easy to find when things were tight.

'Joe Royle was magnificent in the air and he gradually developed an excellent touch. For a spell, he was the best centre-forward in Britain. Alan Whittle came into the

Championship team late on and had a remarkable scoring run. He was quick, alert and sharp in the box.'

Last but not least, Colin turned to his two midfield partners, Alan Ball and Howard Kendall. He said: 'I used to love playing with Bally when he was on blob because he would do some brilliant things. He was my favourite player of that era. I would have happily paid to watch him every week, so to have played alongside him was an honour.

'Howard was a magnificent first-time passer of the ball. He could play it short or sweep it long and was one of the best tacklers I've ever seen.'

On April 1st, 1970, that outstanding Goodison side faced West Brom at Goodison with the title there for the taking. It was to be one of those very special Goodison nights, a 58,000 crowd turning up to see the Blues claim their seventh straight victory — and the Championship crown.

Colin and Alan Whittle were the goalscorers in a 2-0 victory, the *Liverpool Echo* reporting: 'Harvey settled it all midway through the second half with one of the great goals of the season. He collected the ball way out, took it down the left, turned back in his tracks and lost two of his shadowers at the same time.

'He brought the ball into the middle and cracked in a right-foot shot from 25 yards which left the airborne Osbourne helpless. What a goal to clinch the title.'

Colin said: 'It was just hit and miss, but it went into the top corner. We played some great football that night. It was the climax to an amazing season. As a youngster, I had stood in the old Boys' Pen at Goodison and cheered on the Blues. As a young professional in 1963, I had raced back to Goodison from that 'A' team game to see the Championship being won against Fulham.

'I thought at that time, what a magnificent moment it must be for a footballer to win the title and be able to parade the trophy in front of his own fans. It's something you dream about.

'Suddenly I was one of eleven men accepting the

Evertonians don't come any bigger than this pair . . . Everton manager
Colin Harvey and his right-hand man Terry Darracott.

plaudits of the crowd. It was one of the highlights of my
playing career.'

Everton came to within an ace of setting a new points
record that year when it was two for a win. In the wake of
that Albion victory, they beat Sheffield Wednesday 1-0 . . .
sending the Hillsborough outfit into the Second Division.
A win in the final game at Sunderland would have set a
new record of 67 points, but a goalless draw meant the
Blues only equalled the old mark.

Still, the Goodison faithful were more than happy to
settle for the Championship. Along the way, the team had
produced entertaining football of the very highest calibre.

So which was the better of the two sides . . . the 1966 F.A. Cup-winners or the 1970 title giants?

Colin said: 'The 1970 side was the best for a number of reasons. When I played in '66 I was a decent player. I was now more experienced. Alan Ball arrived and improved it and Howard Kendall followed. Tommy Wright had developed his game. We were four years old and better players.'

The lack of success in the years that followed only served to heighten our appreciation of that title team. After playing in more than 380 top-class games for the Blues, Colin Harvey moved to Sheffield Wednesday for £70,000 in 1974. A nagging hip injury finally ended a magnificent career.

It was March 11, 1976 when the news broke that both stunned and saddened all Evertonians. The headline said it all: 'A Goodison God Calls It A Day.'

Thankfully, Colin would soon be resuming his famous links with Everton, progressing through the coaching ranks to become the people's choice as Howard Kendall's successor in 1987.

As a coach and manager he has proved himself a single-minded individual who will work tooth and nail to try and keep Everton at the forefront of English soccer.

As a player, he was truly outstanding. A cutting in the *Liverpool Echo* library, dated December 9, 1972, says everything about Colin Harvey:

'Although slightly built, he could win the ball in tackles with the power and timing of his challenge. He could use it and pass it with immense skill and precision. He could dribble, beat men, shoot, score goals and his work-rate was phenomenal. His sharpness on and off the ball was remarkable.

'To this abundance of football talent he added enthusiasm, a competitive spirit and a whole-hearted dedication which forced him, in every match and training session, to give everything. He does not know how to play it any other way.'

No player could ask for a more colourful testimony to his playing skills than that!

FULL INTERNATIONAL CAP
(England score first)

1961: Malta 1-0.
Total: 1.

CHAPTER SEVEN

Ray Wilson

Back in the sixties, when Goodison Park was the undisputed School of Soccer Science, the fans didn't so much demand skilful football as expect it . . . in all areas of the field.

The Everton motto said it all: Nil Satis Nisi Optimum — Only The Best Will Do!

So when manager Harry Catterick moved in the transfer market in July, 1964, it might seem a little bit strange now that his target was a 29 years old full-back who had spent nine years in the Second Division with his only club — Huddersfield Town.

The fact of the matter is that Ramon Wilson was not your average defender. He was one of those players who destroyed the popular misconception that you had little or no chance of progressing onto an international stage unless you were with one of the game's aristrocrats.

Ray arrived at Goodison Park with 266 League games already under his belt for Huddersfield. More significantly, he had played 30 times for England and was widely regarded as the best left-back in Europe.

So why did he stay for so long in the soccer backwater that is Leeds Road? The answer is quite simple. Ray was brought up in an age when freedom of contract was unheard of. The old phrase 'Soccer Slave' may seem a little dramatic in this day and age, but it was something many of the game's great players had to put up with at that time.

Ambition didn't come into it. Ray explained: 'When you signed for a club in those days, it was for life — unless it suited your employers to sell you. There was absolutely nothing you could do about it. They had you over a barrel.

'The only reason Huddersfield finally let me go to

68

Everton was that I was almost 30 and they decided it was time to cash in. It was the best favour they ever did me.

'It was only when I had been at Goodison for two or three weeks that I began to understand what I'd been missing for the previous 12 years. I'd won 30 international caps, but I had only played in six First Division games.

'My one regret in life is that my career wasn't the other way round. I wish I could have played for Everton from the word go.'

Ray Wilson's story is truly remarkable. He's the lad from the pit village of Shirebrook who became a national hero in 1966 when England beat West Germany to win the World Cup. He was Everton's sole representative in Alf Ramsey's glorious side, Alan Ball being a Blackpool player at that time.

Ray is the soccer star who eventually turned his back on the game he had graced so magnificently to become an undertaker. It seems hard, if not impossible, to relate the world of professional football to that of a Funeral Director. That Ray has been able to take it all in his stride and make a success of the family business says everything about the character of the man.

Derbyshire folk are as down to earth as they come. Ray Wilson has been able to travel down the road of life without changing one jot as a person. For me, he remains the best left-back Everton have ever had, even though he arrived on the Goodison scene so late in his career and subsequently encountered his fair share of injuries.

Wilson was pure class, a point taken up by Terry Darracott who, as a young player, actually made his Everton debut in Ray's number three shirt on April 6, 1968.

Terry recalls: 'He was a brilliant player and a true gentleman. I'll never forget being drafted in to replace him for a game that season when he picked up an injury. Ray was a great influence in the four years he was at Goodison.

'He was an outstanding full-back whose cultured left foot would stick out a mile in any situation. He could also be very strong if the game turned that way.

It's December, 1957, and a young Ray Wilson shows his skill in a Huddersfield shirt. The man trailing in his wake? Could that be a certain Jimmy Hill, playing a good game instead of trying to talk one!

'He could tackle, he was good in the air and he could knock as sweet a pass as you would wish to see from a defender.'

Ray recalls his Everton career with pride. He doesn't see many big games these days, but when he's walking his dogs in the hills above Huddersfield where he owns a little bit of land, he occasionally allows his mind to drift back to those heady times in the sixties when he had the football world at his feet.

Strange as it may seem, he never had any burning ambition to be a professional footballer when he was a lad, explaining: 'I never felt as if I was miles ahead of the other kids of my age in Shirebrook. I grew up in the war years when sport at school was effectively cancelled.

'It was only later in my schoolboy career that I started playing seriously. There was a fantastic amount of organised soccer after the war, but I still never thought in terms of becoming a professional. All through school and during the time I played for the local youth club, I can never remember being asked for a trial.'

Out of the blue, Ray was asked to turn out for an open age side on a day when his youth club had no game. The team lost 6-3, but the youngster with the sweet left foot got all the goals . . . at inside forward. Huddersfield Town asked him to go for a trial and they immediately offered him terms as an apprentice professional.

Ironically, he suddenly received letters from a couple of top clubs, one being Everton who were managed at that time by Cliff Britton. Ray said: 'I decided to accept Huddersfield's offer, just in case the other trials didn't go well and I finished up with nothing. I've never been ambitious in trying to plan my life.

'I've just gone up different roads. In many respects, if you're relaxed, it often works out better. I've never wanted to be a millionaire. Dreams must be attainable.'

The world of football was far from glamorous at that time for the young man from Shirebrook. He recalls: 'It was all so different in those days. Clubs used to have to take three or four team photographs to get everyone on because they would have 40 to 50 players on the ground-staff. The wages were so low that they could afford to keep up the numbers. It made it that much more difficult for a kid to come through the ranks.'

The most staggering thing for Ray was that while Huddersfield had a staff of over 40, he was one of only

A relaxed moment at Bellefield
for Ray Wilson in 1969.

three apprentices. Not surprisingly, the workload was
intense. He said: 'We didn't train with the other players. We
would sweep the terraces, wash the kit, clean the boots —
and then they would give us a ball!

'We were called soccer apprentices, but that probably
contravened the Trades Descriptions Act. It was really
tough trying to break through. I would have been 23 before
I became a first-team regular. I didn't become an
international until I was 25.'

Ray made his League debut in October, 1955. He said:
'Huddersfield were second bottom in the First Division. I
was thrown in against Manchester United who were riding
high at the top on their way to the Championship. I was up
against Johnny Berry, one of the famous Busby Babes.

'There was to be no fairytale ending because they beat
us 3-0. It was a real baptism of fire. We went down that
season. I had played in six games and we lost the lot. It
could have been a destroyer, but I felt an improvement in
my play in every game.'

Ray would eventually play under a manager whose
enthusiasm would prove inspirational . . . the great Bill

Shankly. 'Shanks' became Huddersfield boss after spells with Carlisle, Grimsby and Workington. Ray is one of the few players to have experienced the contrasting managerial talents of Shankly and his great Merseyside rival Harry Catterick.

Ray said: 'Bill's five-a-side games became legendary when he was with Liverpool, but he was exactly the same at Huddersfield. He would keep four Scots back to make up his side and five Englishmen. It was England v Scotland on the asphalt car park at Leeds Road under the mill and the gasometer. We would keep playing until 'Scotland' got in front and that was that.'

Ray had never really thought about the significance of playing for Shankly and Catterick, but he must be in a very select club in that respect. He said: 'I don't suppose there are too many people around who have worked under both men. Johnny Morrissey springs to mind.

'It's amazing how they both achieved success as managers with a completely different approach. People talk about Shankly being a hard man. In my experience, he found it difficult to come down on people. His favourite film star was Jimmy Cagney. He played the role of his hero, although deep down he was not a tough individual himself.

'It was just sheer enthusiasm with Bill, almost a boyish approach to the game he loved. He was inspirational and he knew the game and that's the most important thing.

'By comparison, Harry Catterick WAS tough. He could frighten people to death with his approach. If anyone heard him coming down the stairs at Bellefield, you would see half a dozen senior international players scurrying to get out of the way. He ran the club with an iron fist.

'But the only time you ever saw him in a tracksuit was when the press were about. Even then he had his collar and tie on underneath.'

Ray smiles when he reflects on the Catterick regime. He said: 'He used to lock the training ground gates to keep the fans and the media out. We used to call it Belsen. But you

June, 1964, and Harry Catterick (right) gets his man at last. Ramon Wilson signs on the dotted line for Everton, watched by Mick Meagan, Huddersfield boss Eddie Boot and Goodison secretary Bill Dickinson. Blues full-back Meagan was part of an exchange deal that encouraged Huddersfield to sell.

had to admire Harry in his own way. He was never afraid to take on players with a big reputation.

'Some players can be difficult to handle, but Harry would take them on, no problem. They would soon be brought into line. He used to weigh us every week. We had to clock on every morning. If you were late or overweight, you were fined.'

Yet Ray revelled in every minute of his Everton career. He said: 'The fans had a very special feel for the club. It wasn't a case of four big games a season like I had been used to at Huddersfield. There was a new challenge every week. Every day was a pleasure.'

Ray arrived in a £50,000 deal that took Mick Meagan in the opposite direction. He said: 'My first season was a bit of a let-down to say the least. I played in the opening two games and then picked up an injury that would keep me out for almost four months. I was very disappointed, but the next season was to make up for it in every way.'

Not only did the cultured full-back help Everton to win the F.A. Cup at Sheffield Wednesday's expense, he was to return to Wembley within a matter of months to play his part in England's sensational World Cup triumph.

He said: 'I was knocking 32 and had been a pro for 17 years. During that time I'd never won a thing apart from my international caps. At Huddersfield it had been a regular battle to keep away from the bottom of the Second Division.'

The F.A. Cup run with the Blues was to change all that. Sunderland, Bedford Town, Coventry, Manchester City and Manchester United were all tamed en route to Wembley. Wilson's class, his shrewd use of the ball and his exceptional positional play were as important as the goals scored by the likes of Fred Pickering, Alex Young and Derek Temple.

Ray said: 'We had a very experienced side and we were immediately installed as favourites to beat Wednesday. But they threw everything at us to take the lead. I thought to myself, 'They can't keep coming at us like this.'

'Then they scored again and if it hadn't been for our experience, we would have folded.'

The famous fightback will bever be forgotten. Wilson was absolutely thrilled to have claimed his first major honour, but even in his wildest dreams he couldn't have envisaged what was going to follow in an England shirt.

In the wake of the F.A. Cup Final, World Cup fever

Ouch! Ray Wilson takes a tumble playing for England against Switzerland at Wembley in 1962. He was a Huddersfield player at the time.

began to grip the country, not least on Merseyside where Goodison was to be one of the regional venues.

As soon as the League season was over, Wilson joined up with the England party for a month's get-together at

Lilleshall, followed by a strenuous four-match European tour. Manager Alf Ramsey had no intention of easing his players into the World Cup. He wanted them to be tuned up mentally and physically for the start of the tournament on July 11.

England beat Finland 3-0, Norway 6-1, Denmark 2-0 and Poland 1-0 on that hectic Euro tour, but there was no strain on the players' faces on their return. You don't feel the pressure when you're winning well. I can well remember seeing a news clip of the team coming down the steps of the plane on their return. There was Ray Wilson, smoking a pipe without a care in the world, looking more like a cricket commentator than a footballer who was about to embark on the most exciting few weeks of his life.

England's opening World Cup clash, on Monday, July 11, 1966, was against Uruguay. Ray recalls: 'The South Americans turned out at Wembley with a goalkeeper and ten full-backs! They held us 0-0 and it was as if they had won the trophy itself.'

Ramsey's men now faced Mexico. Manchester United's Bobby Charlton and Liverpool's Roger Hunt scored a goal apiece to set England on their way. The fans now caught the mood and 92,000 turned up at Wembley for the crucial game against France. A Hunt double clinched England a place in the quarter finals and Wilson had a gut feeling that the team could go all the way.

Argentina now blocked England's path. It was to be a sensational match for all the wrong reasons, controversial skipper Rattin becoming the first man ever to be sent off at Wembley. Alf Ramsey called the opposition 'animals' and almost caused a diplomatic incident, but the host nation were in the last four and that was all that mattered.

Ray Wilson remained quietly confident. He said: 'Many people didn't fancy us, but they changed their minds after our semi-final victory over Portugal. Eusebio and his team had been lighting up the crowds at Goodison. At last we were playing a side that wanted to go forward and that suited us.'

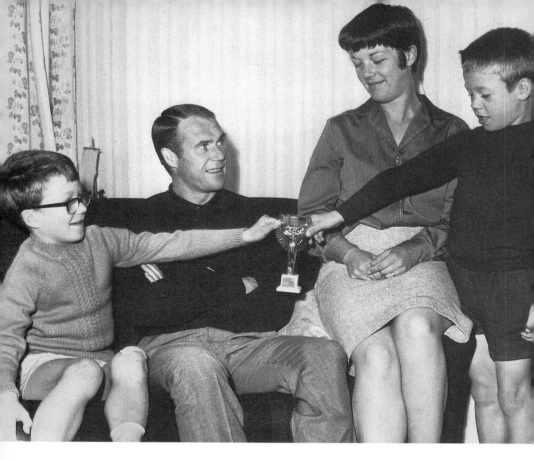

England have won the World Cup and Ray Wilson shows off a replica of the famous Jules Rimet Trophy to sons Russell and Neil, watched by wife Pat.

England 2 Portugal 1 was the final score and a mighty confrontation now loomed on July 30. West Germany stood between Alf Ramsey's men and the Jules Rimet Trophy. For the first time in the tournament, the impeccable Wilson was to experience a moment of genuine personal anguish.

The Final was only 13 minutes old when German star Held floated in an innocuous centre. Everton's England star was so well positioned to clear that nearest opponent Haller never even tried to close him down. But the full-back contrived to head the ball straight to Haller's feet. He immediately shot between goalkeeper Gordon Banks and big Jack Charlton and England were one down.

Ray said: 'It was an awful mistake. The lad had played in

a Third Division ball and I made a marshmallow header down to Haller's feet. Bingo! It was in the net. It looks more horrendous every time I see it.'

At moments like that, experience and outward calm are absolutely vital. Ray simply got on with the job in hand and with England's confidence still sky high, Geoff Hurst equalised inside six minutes. What followed is a part of English football folklore. Martin Peters secured the lead, only for the Germans to equalise through Weber with the very last kick of normal time.

'Ray said: 'It was as dramatic an equaliser as you will see, just seconds before the end. When you've got two equal teams and one comes back like that, you fully expect the other side to drop their heads.

'But we looked much stronger than the West Germans going into extra time. That's a tribute to Alf Ramsey. He was a superb organiser. I can well remember him saying, 'You have won the damn thing once. Now go out and get it won again.' We were determined to do just that.'

The drama was only just beginning. When a Geoff Hurst shot hit the underside of the bar and bounced down, all hell let loose as to whether the ball had crossed the line. The Swiss referee, Herr Dienst, went across to consult his Russian linesman and after what seemed like an age, the goal was given. The great debate continues to this day, although film clips suggest that the whole of the ball did not cross the line.

It didn't matter. Hurst was soon to sprint the length of the field to crash home number four. Ray Wilson shrugs aside the controversy, saying: 'Over the whole game, in terms of controlling it, we fully deserved to win.'

Merseyside united to salute the city's two World Cup stars, Wilson and Roger Hunt. On August 13, 1966, the blue and red hordes packed Goodison Park to witness a unique occasion. Everton, the F.A. Cup holders, played Liverpool, the League Champions, in a very special Charity Shield confrontation.

Wilson and Hunt, holding aloft the Jules Rimet Trophy

A very different
profession for Ray
Wilson in the '80s.
The former England
man is now a Funeral
Director.

and accompanied by club skippers Brian Labone and Ron
Yeats carrying the domestic trophies, led the players on a
lap of honour that inspired a deafening standing ovation.

Ray said: 'I recently saw a picture of myself and Roger
doing that lap of honour. It was a wonderful moment. A lot
of people think Alan Ball was an Everton player during the
World Cup, but I was the only one.

'When you see photographs like that Charity Shield
shot, the memories come flooding back. I'm much more
appreciative of it all now than I was at the time. When
you're playing every week, you take things for granted. It's
like being in the trenches. You get hardened to it.'

Ray Wilson went on to play for Everton in the 1968 F.A.
Cup Final, a losing experience against West Brom. A knee
injury had been troubling him for some time, but he was
still looking forward to the start of the 1968/69 season.
Everton were due to kick off against Manchester United,
the team Ray had made his League debut against for
Huddersfield all those years earlier.

The side had been picked and the polished defender was due to wear his famous number three shirt. He said: 'Harry Catterick wanted to try a couple of dead ball situations on the Friday. I turned and twisted my knee again. I tried to come back as the season progressed, but it never felt right. For someone who had always been quick and who had used that particular strength to get out of different situations, it was very frustrating. I was really struggling and I knew it was the end.'

On May 16, 1969, the *Liverpool Echo* reported that Wilson had been given a free transfer. Manager Catterick was quoted as saying: 'Wilson is one of the finest professionals I have ever known. His behaviour on and off the field is a model to every player. It has been a great pleasure for me to have him on my playing staff and I'm only sorry that he is not years younger so that he could stay at Everton for years to come.'

Ray had been turning on the class for 18 years. He had won 63 England caps. Every single Goodison Park fan was sorry to see him go. If he had joined the Blues as a 19-year-old, instead of a seasoned 29-year-old, he would almost certainly have been one of the all-time greats.

Even so, Ray will be remembered for his cultured skills, his speed of thought and mind and his down-to-earth character.

He has swopped the roar of the crowd for the calm, dignified atmosphere of the funeral parlour which is the family business in Huddersfield.

But beneath the undertaker's coat burns the spirit of '66 . . . football memories that will never die.

FULL INTERNATIONAL CAPS
(England score given first in each case)

1960: Scotland 1-1, Yugoslavia 3-3, Spain 0-3, Hungary 0-2.

1962: Wales 1-1, Northern Ireland 1-1, Scotland 0-2, Austria 3-1, Switzerland 3-1, Peru 4-0, Portugal 2-0, Hungary 1-2, Argentina 3-1, Bulgaria 0-0, Brazil 1-3.

1963: Northern Ireland 3-1, France 1-1, Brazil 1-1, Czechoslovakia 4-2, East Germany 2-1, Switzerland 8-1.

1964: Wales 4-0, Scotland 0-1, Rest of the World 2-1, Uruguay 2-1, Portugal 4-3, Portugal 1-1, Eire 3-1, Brazil 1-5, Argentina 0-1.

1965: Scotland 2-2, Hungary 1-0, Yugoslavia 1-1, West Germany 1-0, Sweden 2-1.

1966: West Germany (sub) 1-0, Wales 0-0, Northern Ireland 2-1, Austria 2-3, Spain 2-0, Poland 1-1, Poland 1-0, Yugoslavia 2-0, Finland 3-0, Denmark 2-0, Uruguay 0-0, Mexico 2-0, France 2-0, Argentina 1-0, Portugal 2-1, West Germany 4-2.

1967: Northern Ireland 2-0, Wales 5-1, Scotland 2-3, Czechoslovakia 0-0, Austria 1-0.

1968: Northern Ireland 2-0, Scotland 1-1, Russia 2-2, Russia 2-0, Spain 1-0, Spain 2-1, Yugoslavia 0-1.

Total: 63.

CHAPTER EIGHT

Alan Ball

Alan Ball was not so much a footballer as a human dynamo. One of his books was entitled *Ball of Fire* and it summed him up perfectly.

He was supremely confident to the point of being arrogant, a 5ft 6inch pocket battleship with the heart of a lion. Bally didn't suffer fools gladly and it often led to confrontation, on the pitch and in the dressing room.

But the man was a football genius, and while individuals — team-mates and rivals alike — might have hated him at any given moment, there was never any doubting their total respect for a player who set standards as high as the moon and who often soared higher than that.

There is no doubt at all that Ball was one of the greatest players ever to wear Everton's royal blue. Signed from Blackpool in 1966 for a then British record fee of £110,000, he transformed the Goodison scene overnight with his infectious enthusiasm and fierce competitive spirit.

A few days before he arrived on Merseyside, Everton had met Liverpool in a no-holds-barred Charity Shield confrontation at Goodison Park, the F.A. Cup holders against the League Champions. The Blues were outplayed in a 1-0 defeat.

Two weeks later, the great rivals met again — this time with Ball in the Everton ranks. The little man scored twice and had a storming game on his home debut as Harry Catterick's men turned the tables on the old enemy in the most emphatic manner imaginable.

From that moment on, Ball was public enemy number one as far as the Liverpudlians were concerned and the ultimate hero in the eyes of the Evertonians. That's the way it would be for five and a half eventful, successful and often controversial seasons.

Ball arrived at Goodison as a World Cup winner, having played his part in England's memorable Wembley triumph over West Germany in the summer of '66. Leeds United boss Don Revie had been tracking him for some considerable time, actually setting up a number of clandestine meetings with the Bloomfield Road star which were strictly illegal, but which summed up the manager's determination to get his man.

Ball was in dispute with Blackpool over his contract at that time and his refusal to sign a new agreement was costing him money. Revie came up with a bizarre plan, encouraging the player to dig his heels in while compensating him with under-the-counter payments which amounted to tapping in the extreme.

The pair would meet on the moors between Manchester and Leeds and on at least three occasions Ball received £100 in cash. Years later, when the England star reflected on the Leeds business in his book *All About A Ball* he was hit hard by the Football Association.

'Revie tapped me for ages,' recalls Allan. 'I got fined for saying that in my autobiography, but it was the truth. Tapping still goes on in football and there's no point in saying any different now. He chased me for ages for Leeds and if I really had any morals about me, I should have gone there because he courted me for a long time.

'But it was just a gut feeling and Harry Catterick got me at the right time. It was a lucky decision because you can make right ones and wrong ones in your life.'

Leeds actually put in a £100,000 bid. Everton offered £10,000 more and when the Elland Road board refused to go any further, the Blues got their man. Revie, it is said, was destroyed by the news.

Whether it was because he had lost a great player or because he had thrown a few quid down the drain is open to debate. All that mattered on Merseyside was that Everton had captured the hottest property in the country. When

In the thick of the action and loving every minute . . . but both Alan Ball and legendary Spurs keeper Pat Jennings missed this Johnny Morrissey cross in March, 1970.

Catterick paraded the new man at Fulham on August 20, 1966, the club's travelling army chanted: 'We've got Alan Ball and we're going to win the League.'

The subject of their optimism responded by plundering a lone-goal winner. In due course, the Championship would be captured and, along the way, Ball would become a Goodison legend.

He said: 'The thing you miss most about football is not being able to play. The things I miss most about Everton and Mersyside are the people. They are probably the only crowd who ever got to me. I played for a great club in Arsenal and a smashing outfit in Southampton as well as playing for Blackpool as a boy, but only one crowd made my head turn and my hair stand on end and that was Everton's.

'You couldn't play badly for them. When I arrived, I had a word with Jimmy Gabriel and he told me I had come to a great club. He said play and they'll love you — or they will find you out!

'It was as simple as that. I made my home debut against Liverpool. We won 3-1 and I scored the first two dead quick. Sometimes you're lucky in life and it goes for you. I think Everton and me were meant to be together. It was a dream start and the fans took to me straight away.

'While I was there, other players came to the club, desperate to do well for the people and yet not quite making it because of their performances. I realised just how fortunate I was because I had three goals in the bag in three games including two in a local derby. All of a sudden they had a new kid on the block and it was me. I couldn't have wished for a better start.'

Ball's incredible appetite for the game, his running, his distribution, his vision — and his refusal to accept anything less than 100 per cent from the players around him — meant that Everton had bought an instant idol. The midfielder struck up a love affair with the fans from the word go.

He was the little man who marched into Goodison like a giant, stamping his authority on the place from the second he walked through the door.

He laughed and said: 'That was my dad in me. He told me that there was never any point in walking in anywhere like a sheep. You walk in like a lion and if you aren't good enough, then you come out like a sheep.'

There were possibly only two men who could put the fear of God into Ball at that time. One was his father, Alan Ball Senior, and the other was his manager, Harry Catterick. The Goodison chief was not intersted in reputations. He was only interested in results.

So what kind of an impression did he make on the new man back in 1966? Alan said: 'He frightened me, but then he frightened everybody. He was basically a very honest man who ruled with a little bit of fear. You only had to be

Mini power pack . . . Alan Ball lets fly.

told off once by him and that was enough. You didn't want it again.'

Catterick had already built one Championship side. He was now building another, determined to maintain Everton's reputation for playing exciting and skilful football.

But if Ball's respect for the manager was total, it was a

hundred times that when it came to his own father. The England star loved and idolised Ball Senior, a man who didn't stand on ceremony if he ever thought young Alan was stepping out of line or getting too big for his boots.

Ball Senior had a solid professional football background, although he never hit the heights as a player or a manager. He turned out for Birmingham, Oldham and Southport and managed the likes of non league Oswestry Town and League outfits Southport, Halifax and Preston.

He was totally dedicated to the game, but more important than that, he was single-minded to the point of being fanatical when it came to his son's football wellbeing. Alan told me a lovely story which summed up their relationship perfectly.

The Everton star was at the height of his fame, a married man and an England player of the highest class, but his form suddenly dipped alarmingly. Ball Senior, manager of Preston at that time, never missed a trick as the Goodison ace was soon to find out.

Alan turned out in a Saturday afternoon home game and didn't play particularly well. In the evening, he travelled over to Manchester with his wife Lesley to have a few drinks at a nightclub called Blinkers.

It was 2.30 in the morning when they finally arrived home. Alan said: 'We had a lovely big house and I can remember walking through the door. The old rocking chair was going and it was my dad. I walked into the room expecting a smile, but all I got was a belt which put me on the floor.

'He said to me, 'Don't you ever waste my time again. What hour is this to be getting in? Get to your bed, go to work, eat your food and you'll be playing well again in a fortnight.'

'He was right. It was a simple remedy and I understood when he said to me, 'You never lose your ability, but you might destroy it if you come in laughing and joking at all hours in the morning.'

'He was the manager of Preston and had told his

Well done pal . . . a young fan with Alan Ball in November, 1971.
Remember the famous white boots?

chairman he was out scouting players. Instead, he had
travelled over to Goodison to watch me play and sort me
out. He was my god!'

Alan was soon back to his brilliant best, the idol of
Goodison and the scourge of Liverpool. Strangely enough,
while the lads on the Anfield Kop loved to hate the Everton

star, a remarkable bond of mutual respect developed between the player and the man who was Mr Liverpool at that time, Bill Shankly.

Alan said: 'What I liked about him was that he was Liverpool-daft, but he appreciated people who were ready to challenge both him and his team. If you stood up and had a crack at Liverpool and didn't go under when he went on and on about the colossal Ron Yeats, the great Ian St. John and the frightening Tommy Smith, he loved you dearly.

'He patted me on the head a few times and I felt very privileged because you knew then that you were tweaking the lion's tail. The greatness of the man was the fact that he wasn't frightened to give praise, even if it was to the so-called worst enemy.

'I was at my peak with Everton and the phone would ring. Suddenly that unmistakable voice would say 'Hello son, how are ye doing?'

'Somehow, he knew your phone number and just wanted to talk about football. He was very special. I've often thought about doing that myself as a manager, ringing up people I admire in other teams, but I'm not quite as fanatical as he was.

It wasn't that he was trying to poach you or anything like that. If he genuinely thought you could play, he was interested in exchanging a few thoughts with you.'

Not that the calls helped Shankly in his ongoing quest to overshadow Everton at that time. Ball played in 13 derbies and was only on the losing side four times.

Harry Catterick never knew about the phone conversations, of course. He would have built the equivalent of the Berlin Wall across Stanley Park if he had known that his greatest star was chatting freely with the leader of the arch-enemy!

Would Alan have fancied playing under Shankly? He told me: 'I would have played for Bill, but only in a blue shirt.'

Enough said. Any suggestion at that time of Bally

Still showing the class as an Arsenal player, shortly after leaving the Blues.

switching his allegiance would have started a civil war on Merseyside. He was the very engine room of the 1970 Championship side, adored by the Goodison faithful for his total commitment and appetite for hard work.

D

So what were his feelings about the challenge ahead on the day he signed for the Blues? He said: 'You walk into Bellefield and you're big time. You put that blue on and the first question they're asking is, 'Can you play?'

'If you can, you're comfortable. If you can't the people will soon let you know because they're so knowledgeable about the game. Harry Catterick put us together . . . Colin Harvey, big Joe Royle, Howard Kendall, Gordon West, Brian Labone and the rest . . . and we took on Liverpool and had a right good time which was lovely for our supporters.

'We played some great football and while you have to give coach Wilf Dixon some credit, a lot of it was off the cuff. We just came together and we used to say we could find each other in the dark. If I had one criticism, it was that the boss split us up too soon. We had just one bad season and he wanted to change his team.'

Just why that famous Championship side failed to go on and dominate English football for years both stunned and shocked not just the Evertonians, but the whole of football.

It was a truly magnificent side and in December, 1969, one of football's most respected figures, Alec Stock of Luton, was asked to assess the Goodison scene. He said: 'For starters, Alan Ball is a player money can't buy. With some stars, you can never tell how they are going to perform from one week to the next. Harry Catterick has no such worries with Alan.

'The Everton manager can wake up every Saturday morning knowing that Alan Ball is going to turn it on. That's why I rate him as the greatest. He has enough skill to satisfy any manager, but he has something else — application. This is his great value to any side. Not so much what he does, but the example he sets. His enthusiasm and wholehearted endeavour rubs off on the other players and he carries them along with him.

'He's in every phase of the game, helping out defenders just outside his own area, grafting in midfield to set up

November, 1974 . . . and Bally has every right to smile. He's just scored for Arsenal against the old enemy — Liverpool.

attacks and then lurking around the opposing penalty area waiting for the half chance. He has control, positional sense, an eye for an opening, energy and determination. Quite simply, he's the best in the business.'

Stock's verdict was spot on. Everyone was singing Ball's praises at that time, not least England's World Cup-winning manager Sir Alf Ramsey. He said: 'A tremendous amount has been written about Ball. They say he's a runner. They say he has fantastic enthusiasm and prodigious strength for a little man and one would not argue with that.

'But what people tend to forget is that Alan Ball is a brilliant footballer.

'He is an ideal player to have in your side because any role he is asked to perform, he will do. I well remember being short of forward players in the Nations Cup competition in 1968 when I took the England team to Madrid to play Spain in the second leg of the quarter finals.

93

I asked Alan to play as a front runner and he gave one of the finest exhibitions of forward play that I have ever seen.

'I knew that Spain would play three central defenders with one working behind the other two. Obviously Ball would be picked up by one of the front two defenders, but it was my hope, and my instruction to Alan, that he should also try to keep the last man occupied.

'He buzzed about in the middle with devastating effect and it was slightly amusing to see two men, each six feet tall, picking up a little man of about 5ft 6ins. Alan occupied those defenders throughout and this played an important part in our eventual victory.'

On the club front between 1968 and 1970, Everton were playing some classical stuff. Alan said: 'I just knew that when we went out on the pitch at Goodison, Anfield, Highbury, Old Trafford, wherever we played, that we were a bit special. The tragedy was when we murdered West Brom in the 1968 F.A. Cup Final and got beat.

'I've never seen so many chances missed in my life in one game of football. It was a sad day for me because we were miles better than them. We had beaten them 2-1 at home and I scored four when we hammered them 6-2 away in the League and then we go and lose 1-0 to them at Wembley. I couldn't believe it because we paralysed them that day.'

The following season, 1968-69, Everton went out of the F.A. Cup in agonising fashion at the semi-final stage to Manchester United and so Ball was denied a golden opportunity to get that Wembley nightmare out of his system.

The Blues finished third in the First Division, but now it was time to go all the way in the League and secure that Championship crown for the first time in seven years.

It was towards the end of the 1970 title-winning campaign that Ball took over as Everton captain. With Brian Labone injured, he led the team for the final eight games during which time they remained unbeaten.

He clearly revelled in the extra responsibility and, during

You can't keep a good man down . . . now in the twilight of his career, but Alan Ball is still the man on the spot, watching Liverpool's Jimmy Case challenge Southampton keeper Peter Wells.

the summer break, it was revealed that he would continue as skipper. His first job was to lead the Champions into a Charity Shield clash against Chelsea and Ball stamped his mark on the game in every way.

He marched out wearing revolutionary white boots and they were to become his trademark for some time. It all seemed quite appropriate, a symbol of his individuality and his very special presence.

But although the Blues won the Shield, Howard Kendall and Alan Whittle scoring in a 2-1 victory, the ensuing season was bitterly disappointing. Everton reached another F.A. Cup semi-final, but a Ball goal couldn't prevent them crashing out to the old enemy, Liverpool.

More significantly, Catterick's side finished a disastrous 14th in the League. Ball, a man whose fiery temper had got him into trouble on many occasions with officials, began to show his frustration with his own team-mates. In the third game, at Elland Road, Leeds, he was involved in a flare-up with full-back Keith Newton after the defender's mistake led to a goal (Everton lost 3-2).

In the following game at Chelsea, he appeared to speak angrily to his midfield partner Howard Kendall after a misunderstanding over the taking of a free-kick. Kendall pushed his captain away and the referee spoke to both players.

The problem was, Ball always demanded impeccably high standards from the people around him, irrespective of his own form. It inevitably led to confrontation on the pitch and in the dressing room.

He said: 'Off the field, I was just an ordinary lad. I loved going down the pub, playing my cribb and going racing. I would always be the first to buy you a drink, but on the park I hated myself.

'I was not a nice person out there because it was my living. My dad brought me up with the attitude that if you are nice, you won't be a great player. He used to say, 'The more they hate you, the better footballer you will be.'

'And that's the way I was, even to my own team-mates. I had so many rows that afterwards I would say, 'What can I do? I'm sorry. Please forgive me.'

'Some people accepted it, others wouldn't give me the time of day. But I wasn't bothered about that because when I played football, I played to win. As I said, you've got to be horrible and do whatever it takes to be successful. If people get upset along the way, then that never worried me very much. My concern was always the club — and the fans.'

Alan was still working like a Trojan in that post-Championship period, but nothing seemed to be going right. At the halfway stage, he had only scored one goal and the team as a whole struggled for form and consistency in a mid-table position. Asked to try a pinpoint reasons for the slump following such a glorious title-winning campaign, Alan says: 'I've never made excuses in my life, but I was one of the first people to have that serious pelvic problem that can actually finish your career. I was having injections and couldn't even lift my legs at times.

'It was during that spell after our League success and I can well remember asking to play sweeper, just to get through games. I wanted to play, but it was a really tough injury and I believe it cost me a year of my life. I had always been lucky with injuries, but this was one you couldn't work with.

'I went on to Arsenal and got goals for them. I moved to Southampton and got goals, but I wasn't right during that particular year at Everton.'

Some people believed that, at the age of 26, Ball had burned himself out with his marathon running in midfield. Arsenal's Bertie Mee begged to differ and on December 22, 1971, he tabled a British record £225,000 bid for the Goodison idol. The news stunned and saddened Evertonians everywhere.

The city was full of rumour and counter-rumour as to why Ball was on his way. Manager Harry Catterick added to the intrigue when he said: 'Aspects of the Ball deal will never be told . . . '

Was it to do with money? Was there a rift between the star player and other members of the squad? I put the question to the man himself and he said: 'Lots of people have asked me this and I'll tell you the dead truth. I came into training one morning and Harry Catterick said he wanted to see me in his office.

'I went up there and he said: 'There's a manager from one of the top clubs in the next room. We've agreed a price, son. You're up for sale.'

'I said to him: 'I don't want to go.'

'He said: 'Son, I've doubled the money I paid for you. We've had six great years. You've done a tremendous job for me and for the club. It will be a great deal for you. Go and earn yourself a few quid.'

'I asked him the name of the manager and he said it was Bertie Mee of Arsenal. They had just won the double and I went on the phone to my dad and told him the gaffer had called me in and told me I was for sale. He said: 'Have you asked him why?' and so I went back to Catterick.

'He said: 'Because it's the right deal for you — and me. Talk to Arsenal.'

'Harry Catterick is dead, God bless him, and only he could tell you why, but that was the reason he gave me and it broke my heart.

'He broke the Championship team up much too quickly and, if he was alive today, I'm sure he would admit it because it got to him and he wasn't very well after that. It's not often that you get people who play for and love a club like we did.'

The admiration and respect was mutual. In the wake of Ball's sensational transfer, an article appeared in one of the papers, written anonymously by a fan. I think part of it is worth reproducing because it summed up perfectly the relationship between the superstar and the people who worshipped him:

'Bally was everything to Everton. He was the undisputed king. Even when things did not go well last season, it just seemed a matter of time until he snappped back into top form. And yet he didn't.

'Every time he touched the ball you hoped that this was going to be the genuine article — the real Ball who had thrilled you for so long. And yet it wasn't.

'Still, if he wants to go, let him. It was good while it lasted. In years to come it will be the good times that stick out. The sheer arrogance of the man, the indefatigable desire to be the best that generated itself throughout the team.

'He was a giant in victory and a larger than life figure in defeat. Until the final whistle, the sight of this small terrier with a number eight on his jersey, running around like a man possessed, is an image that will stay with Evertonians till they die.

'Opponents hated him. But that just made it all the better for you. Watching defenders panic at the sight of him moving towards them: listening to crowds abusing him to reach greater heights. It was a magnificent time to live. It was a thrill to be committed to Everton — and Ball.

'Suddenly, unbelievably, it's over. You went to bed on Tuesday with a poster of Alan Ball on your wall and you woke up on Wednesday morning to find that there was a traitor in your room.

'Bally was Everton. He was part of the family. Now he has gone and we've lost a friend.'

Those words were clearly written from the heart and they sum up perfectly what Alan Ball meant to the fans, not only on the Gwladys Street terraces, but to supporters in every corner of Goodison Park. He was a very special player in a very special team . . . a bundle of dynamite.

FULL INTERNATIONAL CAPS
(England score given first in each case)

1965: Yugoslavia 1-1, West Germany 1-0, Sweden 2-1.
1966: Scotland 4-3, Spain 2-0, Finland 3-0, Denmark 2-0, Uruguay 0-0, Argentina 1-0, Poland 1-1, West Germany 1-0, West Germany 4-2, Poland 1-1, Poland 1-0.
1967: Wales 5-1, Scotland 2-3, Northern Ireland 2-0, Austria 1-0, Czechoslovakia 0-0, Spain 2-0.
1968: Wales 3-0, Scotland 1-1, Russia 2-2, Spain 1-0, Spain 2-1, Yugoslavia 0-1, West Germany 0-1.
1969: Northern Ireland 3-1, Wales 2-1, Rumania 0-0, Rumania 1-1, Mexico 0-0, Brazil 1-2, Uruguay 2-1.
1970: Portugal 1-0, Columbia 4-0, Ecuador 2-0, Rumania 1-0, Brazil 0-1, Czechoslovakia (sub) 1-0, West Germany 2-3, Wales 1-1, Scotland 0-0, Belgium 3-1.
1971: Malta 1-0, East Germany 3-1, Greece 2-0, Malta (sub) 5-0, Northern Ireland 1-0, Scotland 3-1.
1972: Switzerland 1-1, Greece 2-0, West Germany 1-3, West Germany 0-0, Scotland 1-0.
1973: Wales 1-0, Wales 1-1, Wales 3-0, Yugoslavia 1-1, Scotland 5-0, Scotland 1-0, Czechoslovakia 1-1, Northern Ireland 2-1, Poland 0-2.
1974: Portugal (sub) 0-0.
1975: West Germany 2-0, Cyprus 5-0, Cyprus 1-0, Northern Ireland 0-0, Wales 2-2, Scotland 5-1.
Total: 72.

CHAPTER NINE

Howard Kendall

Ask any Goodison Park supporter to name the greatest Everton player of all time and 99 out of a hundred would back that goalscoring legend Dixie Dean.

Ask Blues' fans to nominate their most outstanding post-war star and I suggest a majority verdict might go the way of that pocket dynamo Alan Ball.

But widen the great debate to find the most influential character — on and off the pitch — and you will be struggling to come up with a better candidate than Howard Kendall.

As a player he was a winner in every sense of the word and a key figure in that famous 1970 Championship-winning side. As a manager, his record speaks for itself. He is a member of that very select band of individuals who have both played in and managed Championship teams.

I can only think of nine people in English football who have achieved this very special feat . . . Ted Drake (Arsenal player/Chelsea manager), Bill Nicholson (Tottenham), Joe Mercer (Everton and Arsenal player/Manchester City manager), Alf Ramsey (Tottenham player/Ipswich manager), Dave Mackay (Tottenham player/Derby County manager), Bob Paisley (Liverpool), Kenny Dalglish (Liverpool), George Graham (Arsenal) — and Howard Kendall.

The lad from Crawcrook in the North East has been capturing headlines throughout a memorable career, ever since he became the youngest player ever to appear in an F.A. Cup Final when he turned out for Preston North End in 1964, 20 days before his eighteenth birthday.

Evertonians will remember Kendall for many different things, but for me, his single most important achievement

Kendall the England Under-23 international. How he failed to win a full cap remains one of the great soccer mysteries.

was to finally break Liverpool's stranglehold on the game's top honours. Under Kendall, the Goodison faithful were able to walk tall again.

Even the Liverpudlians appreciated it because the balance of power on Merseyside had gone too far. The verbal banter was all one way.

Kendall changed all that with dedication, total self-belief and a tunnel vision that kept him battling on through those dark days at the back end of 1983 when a section of the crowd even called for his head as he struggled to find a winning blend, walking that tantalising narrow line between success and failure.

Back in the Sixties, Evertonians used to roar out a battle hymn that was barbed, yet sung with a sense of mischief rather than malice. It was aimed, tongue-in-cheek, at those great rivals from across Stanley Park . . .

'Oh we hate Bill Shankly and we hate St. John
And most of all we hate big Ron
And we'll hang the Kopites one by one
On the banks of the royal blue Mersey.'

Going into the eighties, it had almost reached the point at which the famous river was in danger of being re-named the Red Sea! Thanks to Kendall, the Mersey was very much royal blue again — in the football sense, of course — between 1984 and 1987.

Everton won two League titles. They played their part in an unforgettable all-Merseyside Milk Cup Final against Liverpool. They went to Wembley three times on the trot in the F.A. Cup (winning soccer's most famous trophy at the expense of Watford). They claimed the European Cup Winners Cup by beating Rapid Vienna in Rotterdam, and during this glittering spell Kendall was rewarded with two Manager of the Year awards.

No wonder Athletic Bilbao cast envious Spanish eyes towards Goodison Park in the summer of 1987. Kendall's decision to leave the English Champions and join the Basque outfit was a stunner in every sense of the word, a blow softened only by the fact that his inspirational coaching lieutenant and former midfield playing partner Colin Harvey was waiting in the wings, ready and willing to commandeer the Goodison hot-seat.

But this book is not meant to be about managers. It's a celebration of Everton playing greats since the late Fifties. That Kendall and Harvey both qualify in their own right on

Howard Kendall with the Manager of the Year Trophy, shortly before his move to Spain.

that score says everything about their leadership qualities and all-round ability.

The Ball-Harvey-Kendall midfield triumvirate, the engine room of the 1970 title-winning side, will never be forgotten. Yet Kendall himself is quick to play down the legend. He explained: 'The three of us won a lot of the headlines at that time. We were always being singled out by the media and I can well remember Brian Labone picking up a newspaper and joking 'Los Tres Magnificos Again! The rest of us weren't there'.

'It was a tongue-in-cheek comment, but a very good point. We won the Championship that year because we were a good team in all departments. From the early part of 1969 we felt we were the best team in the League and when we finally clinched the title it was an unbelievable feeling.'

As Kendall clutched his Championship medal, his mind inevitably drifted back to those early days when his father Jack coaxed and cajoled him to work hard on all aspects of his game in soccer-mad Ryton-on-Tyne.

Howard was born on May 22, 1946, and as soon as he was old enough to walk, he had a ball at his feet. By the time he was eight, he was playing for the Under 11 side at Usworth Junior School. On his 13th birthday he was selected for the Chester-le-Street district team. He went on to captain Durham County, and an England schoolboy cap followed.

As a Preston player, he was to lead the England Youth team in the 'Little World Cup' in Holland. As an Everton player, he gained an England Under 23 cap and yet Kendall was never able to take the final step on the international ladder.

It remains one of the great mysteries of soccer as to why this outstanding individual, possessing all the qualities to perform at the very highest level on any stage in the world, was never picked for England's senior side.

Not that you will ever hear him bemoaning the fact. Kendall's football life has been so full and varied that he has never had time to dwell on individual disappointments for too long.

His schoolboy potential had attracted such clubs as Arsenal, Birmingham, Middlesbrough and the two teams who vied for his early loyalty as a fan — Sunderland and Newcastle United. His first football shirt sported the red and white stripes of Sunderland, but he began to follow the fortunes of Newcastle because his cousin Harry Taylor had signed for the club.

Howard said: 'Harry's father was blind, but my dad would go to games with him and commentate on the action. I would go along as well and so my early allegiance was with Newcastle.'

The Geordie giants would eventually try to persuade

Concentration in the dug out . . . Kendall the manager with Colin Harvey, former club physio John Clinkard and Gary Stevens (now with Glasgow Rangers).

young Kendall to join them, but Preston had shown interest from the word go and their scout, Reg Keating, had extracted a promise from the family that no decision would be taken prior to a fact-finding mission to Deepdale.

Howard said: 'I was due to visit Arsenal at that time, but my mum and dad agreed for me to visit the Preston set-up, simply because they thought we would be able to pick holes in it and turn North End down.

'But they gave us a great welcome, showed me the digs where I would live and introduced me to a lovely family. It was a big decision for my mother and father to let me go, but they wanted what was best for me and I became an apprentice at Deepdale.'

It was August, 1961, when 15 years old Kendall began his football career in earnest. Two years later he became a full-time professional, by which time his parents had moved to Lancashire from the North East to give him every support. On May 11, 1963, eleven days before his 17th birthday, he was handed a dream debut. It was against Newcastle, the team he had supported as a lad.

He recalls: 'In those days, they would pin all the teams on the notice board. I looked for my name as usual in the reserves and when it wasn't there I thought I must be playing for the 'B' team. It was the other way round and it was a tremendous feeling when I ran out at St. James' Park.'

Fittingly, perhaps, the game finished in an honourable 2-2 draw. Kendall was on his way and less than a year later his name would be splashed across the back page of every newspaper in the land when he found himself named in Preston's F.A. Cup Final side, almost on the eve of the Wembley Final against West Ham.

It was sensational on two counts. Firstly, Kendall would be the youngest ever finalist at 17 years and 345 days. Secondly, he was included because Ian Davidson was dropped for a serious breach of club discipline.

Explaining the decision, Preston chairman Allan Harrison said: 'Davidson was chosen to play in the home game against Northampton, but was given leave of absence by the manager on the Friday after asking to be allowed to attend a funeral in Edinburgh the following day. The reasons Davidson had given were found to be untrue. The manager reported the facts to the board and in view of the circumstances, there was no option but to suspend the player.'

Manager Jimmy Milne revealed that the funeral story was fictitious and that Davidson had admitted as much. On being pressed, the player had changed his story and said that he had gone to Edinburgh to help out a relative who was in debt.

Kendall was naturally elated to be included in Preston's Final line-up, but he was shattered for Davidson — irrespective of the reasons for his omission. He said: 'Ian had earned the right to play at Wembley. He was gutted in every sense of the word. I can remember that every

Perpetual motion . . . Howard Kendall in full flight.

member of the team was presented with a rocking chair before the final. I said to him 'It's yours.'

'He had earned it and it was a tearful experience in every way. I felt for him first of all.

'It didn't really sink in that I was playing, but I think the whole business possibly helped the rest of the team. They were more concerned about me than worrying about their own individual performances.

'People were chasing me for all kinds of photographs. They wanted to picture me in bed on the morning of the match and having my breakfast. Strangely, I didn't feel the pressure. I was too young.

'We were also the underdogs and not expected to win. My only thought was that I didn't want to let anybody down.'

The talented young wing half was never going to do that. In the end, there was to be no fairytale ending, but the Final was a memorable one, finishing 3-2 in West Ham's favour. The Londoners won it in the dying moments, but a newspaper headline said it all: 'Preston lost the Cup, but discovered a star — 17 years old Kendall.'

Howard now set his sights on nailing down a regular place. His next priority was to try and help Preston return to the First Division. The following season was to be bitterly disappointing in the promotion stakes, North End finishing midway in the table. Season 1965/66 proved to be even more frustrating, the club ending up nearer the relegation zone than the promotion frame.

Kendall was impatient for success. He wanted to play for England. He wanted to taste life in the top flight. He wanted everything that every young and ambitious player yearns for. His dreams were clearly not going to be achieved by staying at Deepdale.

The player became increasingly unsettled when his name began to be linked with Liverpool and a number of other leading clubs. Kendall discussed the situation with his father and they decided it was time to put in a transfer request.

Flying tackle . . . a lunging challenge from Kendall at Goodison Park.

In October, 1966, the *Liverpool Echo* reported that the Anfield outfit had put in a bid, only to be told that the young star was not available. In the same breath, Preston told Liverpool's chairman of the day, Mr Sydney Reakes, that the Reds would be kept informed if there was a change of heart.

Within a matter of days, the North End board issued another statement, officially turning down the player's transfer request. Kendall's response was to slap in yet another written request to emphasise his determination to get away. It was to develop into something of a saga, the great debate unfolding in the local and national press. Once again the club dug their heels in.

Howard said: 'Preston had been brilliant to me, but I desperately wanted to make the breakthrough into the First Division. I could understand their reaction and that of the fans, particularly when Liverpool's name was continually mentioned. They had lost so many players to Anfield, men like Peter Thompson, Gordon Milne and Davie Wilson. They didn't want to be looked on as a nursery club for Liverpool.'

It reached the stage at which the Deepdale crowd even took to chanting 'Stay Away Shankly.'

The irony was that when the big move finally came, it wasn't Liverpool, but Everton who pulled off a major coup. Blues' boss Harry Catterick was renowned for his secretive moves in the transfer market. In March, 1967, he clinched an £80,000 deal that left the great Bill Shankly furious.

Howard said: 'I will never forget the night it all happened. Manager Jimmy Milne suddenly appeared at our door, saying that he had a club for me. Immediately, my father said 'Liverpool.'

'Mr Milne said 'No, across the park.' I had never even thought about Everton because their name had never come up in the papers. I was told that Harry Catterick and chief scout Harry Cook were waiting to see me and that I was to get into a car and attend a meeting. I was impressed with Catterick.

'Alan Ball had just signed for Everton. The club had won the Cup the season before and they had some tremendous international players. I had actually seen them beat Sheffield Wednesday at Wembley. I supported them that day because they were a North West team. I didn't make an

Kendall was brave and totally committed. Here he wins the ball against Ipswich.

immediate decision, agreeing to look around the club the next day.'

There were reports at that time of a secret late bid from another club — not Liverpool. Howard revealed that it was Stoke City, saying 'They offered me a much better contract. Alan Ball's father was on the Stoke coaching staff at the time and he was involved in the secret negotiations we were having with Potters' manager Tony Waddington.

'My father asked to speak to Alan's dad and asked him a very pertinent question. 'If Stoke is the right move for my lad, why didn't your lad go there?'

'I thought that was brilliant. It was settled at that moment in time that I would be joining Everton.'

Catterick was delighted to have clinched the deal, stealing Kendall from the grasp of Stoke and out-foxing Liverpool. Bill Shankly was not a happy man, saying: 'All we asked was to be kept informed, but Preston didn't give us a chance.'

The whole affair gave an extra edge to a thrilling F.A. Cup fifth-round tie between the two Merseyside rivals which unfolded at Goodison. Kendall couldn't play in the game, but he watched from the stands as Alan Ball plundered a memorable winner.

Before the game, the crowd had recognised their new signing and they gave him a tremendous ovation. Kendall's debut came in the home League game against Southampton on March 18, 1967. In his own words, it was a 'nightmare'.

He said: 'We lost 1-0 and I didn't play well. I just wanted to sneak away, but I had to stop in a local garage for some petrol. Suddenly, a couple of Evertonians appeared and when they saw me, one fan put his coat over a puddle in front of me. Another was waving his arms and bowing down. I thought, 'If this is what they do when you have a nightmare, what will it be like if I actually play well?'

'It was smashing to be accepted by them and to be part of a great club.'

Howard's appearances at the back end of that season were to be restricted by injury, but he was soon forging a tremendous uderstanding in midfield with Ball and Colin Harvey . . . Los Tres Magnificos!

The 1967/68 season saw Everton begin to develop as a potent force. Howard said: 'We played some great stuff, possibly even better than in our Championship year, but we lacked consistency.'

The season ended at Wembley, another losing experience for Kendall. This time West Brom were in opposition and a Jeff Astle goal made a mockery of all the pre-match predictions.

Everton continued to develop as a side. Gordon West was supreme in goal, Brian Labone a giant in the heart of the defence, Johnny Morrissey a tenacious and skilful winger and Joe Royle a powerful target man up front. The Blues finished third at the end of that 1968/69 campaign and also reached the semi-final of the F.A. Cup, but second best is never good enough on Merseyside.

Manager Harry Catterick demanded and got the very best out of his players and Everton embarked on a Championship year in which football of the very highest class was served up to a receptive Goodison audience.

Howard said: 'It was just a case of believing we were the best in the country and of being on the same wavelength as the other players on the field. We just seemed to gel perfectly.'

As for the Ball-Harvey-Kendall partnership, Howard said: 'We were different types and contributed in different ways. At that time, if you won the midfield, then you won your games. Now, if you've got quality strikers you win matches. We took much of the limelight, but we had world-class defenders at the back and super strikers up front. It was a team effort in every sense.'

Incredibly, the team that looked capable of dominating the Seventies suffered an inexplicable fall from grace. From being first, they dropped to 14th, 15th and 17th in successive seasons. Howard said: We just fell away and it was so disappointing, especially after the way we had played to win the title. Injuries played a big part. At the same time, Alan Ball's goals dried up. From scoring a bundle in the Championship year, he dropped to two the following season. He became unsettled and, for a number of reasons, we failed to fulfil our potential.'

Despite the ups and downs, Kendall's own level of play very rarely fell below top class. He took on the captaincy and when he chalked up his 200th Everton League game against Coventry City in December, 1972, the Sky Blues general manager Joe Mercer — a former Goodison giant himself — was moved to say: 'I'm tired of telling people that Kendall is still the best wing half in England.'

The knowledgeable sporting public of Merseyside

agreed and on January 26, 1973, the Everton skipper became the very first winner of the *Liverpool Echo's* prestigious Sports Personality of the Year award. Three Anfield giants finished behind him in the poll in the shape of Emlyn Hughes, Kevin Keegan and Bill Shankly.

It was a sad day for all Evertonians when Kendall finally moved on to a new challenge in February, 1974, the bait used by new Blues' boss Billy Bingham to capture Birmingham City striker Bob Latchford.

Like General McArthur, Kendall would return. He moved from St. Andrews to Stoke, the club that had tried to sign him all those years earlier, and his coaching skills surfaced under the astute guidance of Alan Durban.

He took the player/manager's job at Blackburn Rovers and gained them promotion to the Second Division. The wheel turned full circle when he was charged with the task of reviving Everton's flagging fortunes going into the 1981/82 season.

His subsequent managerial triumphs would fill a book in their own right. Quite simply, Kendall put the life blood back into the Blues. Success didn't just fall into his lap. He had to work hard for it.

He never ducked difficult issues, always preferring to stand his ground and explain his own point of view. Kendall remains one of the game's great communicators, the difference being that he can talk the hind leg off a donkey in Spanish as well as English these days.

In many respects, it's rather appropriate because at the peak of his playing career, he had all the assurance and timing of a matador.

He was dynamic in every way. His running was powerful, his passing accurate, his positional play exceptional and his commitment total. He was brave in the tackle to the detriment of his own safety at times, but perhaps his greatest quality was his consistency. He set himself very high standards and worked tirelessly to make things happen — week in, week out.

You get out of life what you put in. Howard Kendall bowed out with the Championship trophy standing proudly in the Goodison Park board room for the second time in three years. He was a winner right to the end.

CHAPTER TEN

Bob Latchford

If you want to bring a smile to the face of any Evertonian, ask him about the significance of Saturday, April 29, 1978.

The Blues didn't win a Championship or a Cup that day, but the wall of sound that swamped the players in the wake of the final home League game of the season against Chelsea said everything about an unforgettable occasion.

The 6-0 scoreline was impressive enough, but the day belonged to one man . . . free-scoring striker Bob Latchford. He went into the game needing to score twice to become the first top-flight player for six years to plunder 30 League goals.

Over 43,000 supporters turned up, all willing big Bob to produce the goods and claim a £10,000 prize being offered by a national newspaper. The match proved to be sensational, to say the least.

The powerful centre-forward will never forget that afternoon when Goodison went goal-crazy and he was the toast of Merseyside. He said: 'There was quite an atmosphere that day, considering there wasn't very much on the game itself. The pitch was dry and bobbly, but the goals soon started to flow.'

The only problem was, the Blues swept into a commanding 3-0 lead without Latchford hitting the target. Was it going to be one of those days? The man himself suddenly provided the answer with a second-half header that produced a deafening roar of elation from the crowd. The target was now within his grasp and the fans went wild every time the Blues crossed the halfway line.

Bob's team mate, Mike Lyons, will never forget the closing stages of the game. He said: 'I scored the fifth goal,

Soccer history is made. Bob Latchford signs on for Everton for £350,000, watched by delighted manager Billy Bingham and Alan Waterworth.

tucking the ball into the bottom corner. I turned away to celebrate, but because I hadn't knocked the ball back to Latch who was in a great position, everybody just stood and looked at me.'

Mike smiled and said: 'It's the only time I've scored at Goodison and felt sick about it!'

But Bob would not be denied that magical 30th strike. His moment of glory came from the penalty spot and the place simply erupted. He said: 'It was a terrific moment, a fantastic way to end the season.'

To all intents and purposes, Everton's number nine had hit the jackpot in a big way by securing that £10,000 prize. In reality, the money was meaningless in terms of his own bank account. Part of the deal was that £5,000 would go to the Football League and Professional Footballers Association Benevolent Funds. Bob decided to share the rest between all of the men who had helped him to achieve his 30-goal haul.

Everybody received the princely sum of £192. Bob said: 'The crazy thing was that I actually got taxed on the basis that I had received £5,000 and it took me three or four years, wrangling with the Tax Office, to sort it out. If I'd known, I would have told them to keep the damn money!'

Opposing defenders would have taken some smug satisfaction from Bob's prize headache. After all, had he not taxed THEM to the limit, year in, year out, with his remarkable goalscoring prowess?

Bob had that special knack of turning half chances into goals. He was the master of the near-post header and was Everton's leading League scorer for four seasons between 1974 and 1978.

In his eight seasons at Goodison, he more than repaid the British record fee of £350,000 that Everton forked out for his services. Brought up in Birmingham, Latchford attended Brandwood School in Kings Heath. He played as a wing half at junior level and actually signed for Birmingham City as an outside-left in 1966.

It's hard to imagine Bob as a flying winger, but he laughed and said: 'I had a bit of pace as a 15-year-old, although they quickly moved me into the middle.'

The St. Andrews outfit soon realised they had a real goal machine in their midst and on March 21, 1969, they gave young Latchford his Football League debut against Preston North End.

He recalls: 'It was a very wet and cold Tuesday evening. The pitch was muddy, but we won 3-2 and I scored with two headers, one in each half. Fred Pickering, the old Everton centre-forward, played centre-half for Birmingham that night.'

Latchford could not have asked for a more encouraging start to his League career, but he realised very quickly just how tough it was trying to score goals consistently at that level. He said: 'It's never easy, especially when you're a local lad and things aren't going too well. It was only when

Super salute . . . Latchford takes a bow after a magnificent Goodison Park display against his old club Birmingham.

Fred Goodwin took over as manager that things began to change for me.

'He got hold of me and turned me into a player by forcing me to go back to basics. It was Fred who groomed me into a top-class forward. We had a great striking force at that time with a young Trevor Francis coming through. Gordon Taylor, the current PFA boss, was providing the crosses and Bob Hatton, my attacking partner, was a constant threat to opposing defences.

'As a team, we scored lots of goals, but we were just as likely to let them in at the other end. Fortunately, we scored more than we conceded. Hatton was a great pro and very underrated. He possibly deserved a chance to prove himself at some sort of international level.

'As for Trevor Francis, he was sensational — even when he was just 16. He was like lightning and could pick the ball up and run straight at goal. More often than not the ball would end up in the net. He was also strong in the air, a phenomenal talent.'

Francis, of course, developed into a world-class star. He won a European Cup winner's medal with Nottingham Forest and proved he could match the best on the Continent with Italian outfit Sampdoria. Rival managers couldn't fail to be impressed by Birmingham's striking talent in those early days, taking particular note of Latchford's scoring ability.

He had hit the target 68 times in 158 appearances for the Midlands outfit when Everton's Billy Bingham moved in for him in 1974.

The Blues were so keen to clinch the deal, they offered midfielder Howard Kendall (valued at £180,000), full-back Archie Styles (£90,000) and £80,000 in cash.

The £350,000 smashed the existing British record, putting the £250,000 Derby County paid to Leicester for defender David Nish firmly in the shade. Birmingham were also given an option on that great Goodison centre-forward Joe Royle, dependent on whether the player wanted to leave later in the season. Bingham was clearly ready to pull out all the stops to get his man.

Bob said: 'Every player wants to play for a big club. Everton are big in every way, very professional on and off the field. For the first few months I felt the pressure of that transfer fee, but once I settled in and started scoring regularly it lifted and I never thought about it again.'

The powerful centre-forward only had the chance to figure in 13 games towards the end of that first season, 1973/74, but he still managed a goal every other game. The Blues finished seventh. They improved to fourth the following season when Latchford bagged 17 League goals in 36 games, but finished a disappointing 11th in 1975/76.

Classic header . . . Latchford bullets the ball towards goal in a clash against Derby County.

The pressure was beginning to mount on boss Bingham to produce the goods. That '75/76 campaign was to be a difficult one, for manager and centre-forward. Bob was going through a lean spell and Bingham dropped him for the League visit to Stoke in November. The star striker was soon recalled, but in February he was forced onto the sidelines again — this time with cartilage trouble.

At the same time, he was becoming increasingly frustrated with his financial situation, soaring inflation biting into his wages. He had not had a rise for three years and felt the only way out was a transfer. Bingham resolutely refused to listen to any such talk and Bob got his head down, scoring twice on the opening day of the '76/77 season at QPR. No one could have anticipated the events of the next few months, Bingham losing his job with Everton on the Wembley trail in the League Cup.

The crunch date was January 10, 1987. Ironically the manager had just bolstered the side with two big signings.

Duncan McKenzie arrived from Anderlecht and Bruce Rioch from Derby County, but with the club 13th in the table and the Championship effectively out of reach, Gordon Lee was brought in from Newcastle United to try and revitalise matters.

Bob said: 'They were two very different managers. Billy was quite a taskmaster. It was always noses to the grind-stone with him. He had this fear about Liverpool and their success. We always seemed to train twice as hard in 'derby' weeks under Billy. I suppose both men suffered because of Liverpool's ongoing success, but things were a little bit more relaxed under Gordon — even though his whole life revolved around football.

'Try to talk to him about anything else and you were wasting your time. He loved and backed his players and you had to have total respect for him because of that.'

Lee's enthusiasm, but more significantly a crucial second-leg goal from Latchford, helped Everton to see off Bolton in the League Cup semi-final. The catchphrase of the day was 'Everton Are Magic' and it was with supreme confidence that the team approached the Wembley final against Aston Villa. Sadly, a goalless draw on the big day proved to be something of an anti-climax for both sides and two marathon replays were about to unfold, first at Hillsborough and then Old Trafford.

Latchford scored, both in Sheffield and Manchester, but still found himself on the losing side at the end of the day. A Brian Little double and a Chris Nicholl effort finally secured Villa a 3-2 win — and the Cup.

It was to be bitter Cup disappointment for Everton all the way that season, the Blues losing out to arch-rivals Liverpool in the semi-final of the F.A. Cup, once again after a replay. Bob didn't figure against the Reds, recalling: 'I got injured the previous week when I turned my ankle on Derby County's infamous pitch.'

He had to watch in despair like every other frustrated

Merseyside Sports Personality of the Year for 1977 . . . Bob, pictured with *Liverpool Echo* Editor of the day, John Pugh.

Evertonian when referee Clive Thomas controversially ruled out what appeared to be a perfectly good Bryan Hamilton goal. Bob said: 'I still believe we were robbed. Thomas wouldn't say why he disallowed it. Bryan wasn't offside and if the decision was for a handling offence, the ball came off the top of his thigh. It was so frustrating because we were playing as well as any team that year.

'Liverpool were not at their best that day and we threw a couple of goals away. We should have beaten them in that first game and they knew it. I don't know how much it affected us, but we lost the replay 3-0.'

E

Once again, Everton had been the nearly men. Bob said: 'That was a good way to describe us. I always felt that we were a couple of quality players short in the chase for honours. We were never quite able to grasp the final chance. I look back at Villa in the League Cup. We were well capable of beating them, but just didn't grasp it. It was my one and only Cup Final and it would have been nice to have finished up with a winner's medal, especially after scoring in both replays.

'I've mentioned the Liverpool semi-final and then there was another bitterly disappointing night three seasons later when we went out to West Ham at the same stage after a replay. I scored in that game as well, but we lost 2-1 at Elland Road. It should never have come to that. We should have beaten them at Villa Park, but Brian Kidd was sent off and it upset the balance of the team.

'When I look back at my time at Everton, we finished third in the League in 1978 and also managed fourth place twice. We reached Wembley in the League Cup and figured in two F.A. Cup semi-finals. It would have been a good record at most clubs, one to be proud of. But for Everton it wasn't good enough at all. You go to a big club to be first and win trophies. The fans at Goodison expect and deserve success.

'We never achieved it in my time because we didn't have that all-important strength in depth. But we did have some exceptional individual players, men like Dave Thomas who helped me score those 30 goals in 1977/78. He was a very good winger with two good feet and good balance. He always wore boots with rubber studs, whatever the conditions. His crosses were inch-perfect and I'm sure a player like Graeme Sharp would love to have him about today. Dave was very direct, always going for the by-line and getting in excellent centres.'

With Thomas providing the ammunition, Mike Lyons battling away in defence with Mike Pejic, Martin Dobson showing his class in midfield and Andy King and Duncan McKenzie delighting the fans with their skill and unquestionable ability, Latchford revelled in that '77/78 season.

In February, the city's sporting public voted the Everton centre-forward the *Liverpool Echo* Merseyside Sports Personality of the Year. A few months earlier, Bob had gained the first of 12 England caps — playing in a World Cup qualifier against Italy at Wembley. His selection was long overdue, but perhaps that made it all the sweeter.

It had been virtually impossible to overlook his stunning form. When Everton trounced QPR 5-1 at Loftus Road in October, Latchford plundered four goals. A newspaper headline said it all . . . 'Best In The Country!'

He gave central defenders David Needham and Ron Abbott a terrible time in that game. Bob scored with a diving header after eight minutes, King providing the killer pass. Thomas, almost inevitably, was the provider when the striker dived in for his second after 18 minutes. Manager Lee later enthused: 'That was the kind of goal I was dreaming about when I bought Thomas. Latchford is deadly when he gets the ball in the area at the right time and with the right pace behind it. Thomas can do this for him.'

The hat-trick came when the number nine bundled home another King cross and goal number four followed after 68 minutes, a Lyons shot deflecting over the back four, enabling Bob to pounce again.

The four-goal haul was his best ever in League football, although he did beat it the following season when he scored a stunning five goals in an 8-0 League Cup romp against Wimbledon.

But that '77/78 season was the one that sticks in the memory. When Bob bagged a hat-trick in a free-flowing 6-0 home victory over Coventry in November it was described as 'The match that had everything'.

The *Echo* reported: 'Excitement flowed around the ground like an electric current. Latchford's hat-trick was excellent and Thomas produced some scintillating wing play.'

Lift-off . . . Bob seems to be flying straight into the crowd after a spectacular moment's action against Carlisle.

The centre-forward's goal tally in the League had reached 28 by mid-April. The magical 30 was clearly very much on the cards with three games still to play. It proved to be a hair-raising experience for one Goodison fanatic, a man named Filadelfo la Rocco, known to all and sundry as Rocco.

He was manager of a pizza parlour and restaurant in Prescot and was convinced Bob was going to produce the goods in the penultimate match, an away clash at West Brom. So confident was Rocco that he said he would shave all of his hair off if the striker, his favourite player, missed out.

Incredibly, Everton went down 3-1, George Telfer getting their lone goal. Out came the scissors, a crestfallen Rocco declaring: 'I am a Sicilian and a Sicilian always keeps his word.'

In full flight . . . Bob Latchford closes in for the kill.

Latchford's great moment wasn't delayed for very long. The Chelsea game loomed and that £10,000 prize, offered by the *Daily Express,* was won with a flourish on one of the most memorable afternoons in the history of Everton Football Club.

Bob remained at Everton for three more seasons. Ironically, it ended where it all began when the wheel turned full circle and Howard Kendall, the man involved in that initial exchange deal in 1974, returned to Goodison

Park as manager. Bob was the first to leave as Howard began his great rebuilding job.

The striker who had scored 138 goals in 286 appearances for the Blues said: 'I felt as if I had given as much as I could for seven or eight years in an Everton shirt. I needed a change and decided it would be best if I moved on to allow new blood to come in. I suppose it was strange that Howard's return coincided with my departure and, with hindsight, possibly I made the wrong decision to go.

'But that's football. I still look on Merseyside as my second home. My family were very happy there. If I was looking for somewhere to settle in the future, Merseyside has got a good chance of seeing us.'

Bob Latchford would certainly be welcome. His goals gave Evertonians a great deal of pleasure.

FULL INTERNATIONAL CAPS
(England score given first in each case)

1978: Italy 2-0, Brazil 1-1, Wales 3-1.
1979: Denmark 4-3. Eire 1-1, Czechoslovakia (sub) 1-0, Northern Ireland 4-0, Northern Ireland 2-0, Wales 0-0, Scotland 3-1, Bulgaria 3-0, Austria 3-4.
Total: 12.

CHAPTER ELEVEN

Andy Gray

I'll never forget the day Andy Gray signed for Everton. Nor will I forget the day he left.

It's the story of the 'scoop' that fell into my lap thanks to a sharp-eyed *Liverpool Echo* reader — and the farewell letter from the swashbuckling centre-forward that said everything about his very special relationship with the fans.

November 10, 1983 had the makings of a very run-of-the-mill type of news day in the *Echo* office in Old Hall Street until the phone rang on the Sports Desk at around 10am. A voice at the other end of the line enquired: 'Is Andy Gray signing for Everton today?'

Hand on heart, I told the caller that I didn't know, but that I would check it out. The mystery caller said that he had seen the Aston Villa striker just a few minutes earlier, buying a paper in a newsagents across the road from Goodison.

I was used to this type of call. Someone starts a rumour and within a couple of hours it has swept the city, the tale becoming more colourful with every telling. But the one thing I've learned down the years is that you never dismiss a story out of hand, no matter how outrageous or unlikely.

I would often start my regular morning call to Howard Kendall by saying: 'I know this sounds ridiculous, but . . .'

I duly rang Bellefield and asked for the Everton boss. He wasn't available.

Now Howard was always available, which set the alarm bells ringing in my head. I put in a call to a contact in the Midlands and drew a blank. Maybe it WAS just a hoax call. But then again, maybe Gray was at Goodison.

I was on pins as the noon deadline drew ever closer.

129

Andy Gray turns away after plundering Everton's second goal in the 1984 F.A. Cup Final against Watford.

Howard was still 'unavailable', and so with about 15 minutes of breathing space before the first edition, I rang secretary Jim Greenwood. Did he know where Howard Kendall was?

Now Jim's a wily character, answering my question with one of his own: 'Why do you want to know?' 'I know this sounds ridiculous Jim, but . . .' The momentary silence on the other end of the line told me that something was in the air. Jim neither confirmed nor denied it, telling me to write nothing until Howard contacted me. He promised a call inside ten minutes . . . right on the dreaded deadline.

I alerted the sports desk, sent for Gray's cuttings from the *Echo* library and hammered out a story which I was prepared to ditch if the Everton boss refuted the Gray link. The phone rang and it was Kendall, clearly upset that the cat was out of the bag, but happy for me to break the news — providing I didn't quote him directly.

So thanks to that *Echo* reader, we carried banner headlines that the Blues were about to sign a player who would become one of the inspirational figures behind Everton's great Eighties revival.

Gray's stay at Goodison was to be comparatively short — just 20 months. But during that time the F.A. Cup, the League Championship trophy and the European Cup Winners Cup all adorned the trophy room. The cavalier centre-forward had earned his place amongst the Everton Greats by going in where it hurts, scoring crucial goals and inspiring everyone around him. His power in the air, a confidence that bordered on the arrogant, and his never-say-die approach captured the imagination of the fans who immediately took the Scot to their hearts.

A very special relationship was forged between player and supporters, and just how strong that bond was can be gauged from the letter Andy sent to me on the day he left Goodison Park to return to his first English club, Aston Villa.

He had received hundreds of cards and letters from well wishers and wanted to thank them through the columns of the Echo. His words clearly came from the heart . . .

'My Dear Friends,
And I trust we shall remain so. I received so many cards from you regarding my departure that I felt I must write to thank you all. I have never felt so moved or humble as I did when your letters started to arrive. I knew we were close, but I didn't realise how close.

'I have so much to thank you for over the last two seasons and I am proud to have been part of the Everton revival. The club will always be a special place for me as it gave me two of the happiest years of my life. All I basically want to say to you, to Colin Harvey, Mick Heaton, Terry Darracott and the best bunch of lads I have ever worked with is "Thanks for the memories".

'God Bless You All and may your amazing success continue.

'Your mate forever . . . Andy Gray.'

A sign of the times for Andy Gray after signing for Everton in November, 1983.

It was hard to believe that Andy had gone, transferred to Villa for £150,000 in the wake of two truly remarkable seasons.

In many respects, Gray's signing had been the last throw of the dice for Howard Kendall. The Blues were struggling for form, consistency and results when he arrived, and pressure was mounting on chairman Philip Carter to sack the manager.

Kendall made a very shrewd move when he promoted reserve coach Colin Harvey to first team duties and — almost in the same breath — he swooped for Gray, a striker whose career was going nowhere at Wolves.

As an Aston Villa star, the bold and supremely confident centre-forward had become the first man in history to receive both the Player of the Year and the Young Player of the Year awards in the same season from the Professional Footballers' Association.

He moved to Wolves for a British record fee of £1,469,000, but Kendall was able to secure his services for a much more modest £250,000. Gray recalls: 'I knew that

Everton were much better than their League position suggested. I also knew it was a big club with a lot of potential.

'So I travelled to meet Howard Kendall for a long chat at the 'Queens' pub which is very close to the Bellefield training ground. We had a nice meal and a bottle of wine. He was trying to check me out and I was happy enough to say that I would sign if he could sort everything out with Wolves.

'He wanted me to put pen to paper there and then, but I finished up signing a form for a month's loan until the agreement was sorted out in detail. He didn't have to sell the place to me. Goodison Park is a magnificent ground and I had always enjoyed playing there. I made my debut for Wolves at Goodison and scored in a 3-2 win.

'On the day I arrived, I was introduced to the local press boys and one of them asked me: 'What's going to change?'

'I replied that I had joined Everton to win things and someone said 'We've heard all that before.'

'You haven't heard it from me,' I said, and I think they realised that I was serious.'

Gray was well aware of the importance of the signing for Kendall. He said: 'I was his final shot in many respects. If I had gone wrong, things might have changed for him. If more money had been available at that time, Howard might have gone for someone else. I came into his price range.'

Kendall didn't just buy Gray for his ability, but also for his acknowledged inspirational qualities. Gray realised very quickly that he was carrying a tremendous responsiblity on his shoulders. He said: 'Four years earlier I had moved from Villa to Wolves for £1.5m. I didn't feel one ounce of pressure. I went to Everton for £250,000 and I really did feel it.

'Maybe it was the ghost of the Deans, Lawtons, Royles and Latchfords that added to it. The number nine shirt has always always been very symbolic at Goodison. You can't afford to fail and I had no intention of doing so.

Going in where it hurts . . . the definitive picture of Andy Gray, in action against Doncaster.

'The supporters seemed to take to me straight away. Liverpool reminded me of my native Glasgow. The docks, the river, the people, the humour. It was home from home. We were working hard behind the scenes to get things moving, but it still wasn't happening off the pitch.

'Then, at the turn of the year, we played Stoke City in the third round of the F.A. Cup. Thousands of Evertonians travelled to the Victoria Ground to give us unbelievable support. Howard Kendall felt a team talk was unnecessary. He just opened the dressing room window and let us listen to the singing and chanting of our fans.

'We won 2-0 and I scored one of the goals with a header. Okay, so we'd only beaten Stoke — big deal. But the way we played and the way the fans responded suggested that a change was coming over the club. Things just snowballed from there.'

Andy's only frustration during that eventful 1983/84 season was that he was cup-tied and unavailable for Milk

Cup action. But he was very much involved in the F.A. Cup, not least when he scored an absolutely incredible goal in the quarter final at Notts County. It was a nasty day with the rain sweeping down across Meadow Lane.

The Scottish star produced a remarkable match winner that few strikers would have attempted, let alone steered into the net. The tie was balanced on a knife-edge at 1-1 when the Blues gained a free-kick after 47 minutes. Kevin Sheedy lifted the ball towards the box where it soared over the head of Graeme Sharp and his marker David Hunt. Gray suddenly arrived from nowhere, launching himself along the slippery surface to make an amazing horizontal header.

He made contact a matter of inches above the ground and goalkeeper Mick Leonard had no chance as the ball edged iside the right-hand post. Boss Howard Kendall suggested that Gray had 'rotavated the ground with his nose' as he flung himself at the ball. It was a truly remarkable effort.

Gray wasn't just playing well himself, he was bringing the best out of the men around him, not least striking partner Graeme Sharp. He said: 'Graeme was always associated with spectacular goals, never with the tap-ins from six yards. But that's where most of your goals come from.

'He learned very quickly and his goal rate soared. People said that there was no way we could play together and be a success, but they were wrong. When I arrived at Goodison, a lot of players had the weight of the world on their shoulders. They were bubbling in training, but as soon as we went out onto the park, no one wanted the ball. I tried to boost their confidence in the only way I knew how.

'Suddenly they were seeing this geezer who many believed was past his best going out there and demanding the ball. It began to rub off.

'I can remember my debut against Nottingham Forest. Adrian Heath hadn't been scoring so I pulled him to one side and said, 'You're due a goal. Get close to me in the

Rotavating the ground with his nose . . . Andy Gray's famous diving
header in the Cup against Notts County.

box. Sure enough, the ball came in and he was on the spot
to cash in and claim his first goal of the season.

'Gary Stevens had been struggling in the reserves. He
suddenly burst onto the scene. Peter Reid had been in and
out, but he finally put a run together and became a
tremendous influence on the side. It was a culmination of
things that got us going.

'Colin Harvey's impact also made a difference. I have the
greatest respect for him as a coach. He's also a
tremendous Evertonian. So from being a team frightened
to go out and play, we became a team to be respected. If
we went a goal down, it didn't seem to matter. We always
felt as if we could fight back.'

Everton, with Gray forced to watch from the sidelines,
battled their way to the final of the Milk Cup, losing in a
fiercely contested replay at Maine Road, Manchester to
arch-rivals Liverpool. That defeat only served to make the
players doubly determined to return to Wembley in the
F.A. Cup. Having beaten Stoke, Gillingham, Shrewsbury
and Notts County, they now faced Southampton in a tense
semi-final at Highbury.

The Saints' fans were outnumbered and outshouted, Adrian Heath snatching a lone-goal winner that sparked the most amazing scenes of elation and celebration imaginable. Gray will never forget the day and the coach journey home. He said: 'It was one of the most memorable days of my life. When we were getting changed for the match, the atmosphere was electric.

'You can look down into the street from the dressing room windows. The Evertonians were parading around in their thousands and I spotted ten of my family walking past. I can remember Lawrie McMenemy, the manager of Southampton, saying that he looked at his players and saw nothing but nerves. He looked at us and knew it was going to be one of those days.

'Later, we had an incredible coach journey back to Merseyside. Blue and white scarves were everywhere on the motorway and when the supporters' coaches passed us, the fans would all scramble to one side, banging on the windows, singing, chanting and having a tremendous time. How some of those coaches didn't tumble over because they were so top-heavy on one side I'll never know!'

The great transformation from those tense and frustrating days when Andy first arrived was complete. The powerful striker knew that Everton would soon have their first trophy on the sideboard after 14 barren years, and he was soon to realise just how confident his team mates had become.

He said: 'A couple of days before the Final against Watford, I went on TV with Adrian Heath and Peter Reid to discuss the game. You normally try to be reasonably diplomatic in these interviews and I was talking about some of Watford's strengths and saying what a great occasion it would be.

'Suddenly, Adrian chipped in to say we would win 2-0, no sweat, and Reidy also predicted a confident Everton victory!'

That's the way it would be. Gray scored one of the goals in a 2-0 triumph, Sharp getting the other. As usual, there

Andy Gray crosses his fingers, manager Howard Kendall checks the time . . . and the signing-on forms speed their way to League head-quarters in November, 1983.

was nothing straightforward about Andy's effort. Many people believed he fouled goalkeeper Sherwood when they jumped for the ball in front of the posts, but Andy says: 'The more I look at the video, the more I'm convinced that I didn't touch him. It was pure instinct and the keeper should have collected it. I just put my head there, he fell over and the ball was in the back of the net.'

Everton finished that 83/84 season on the up and up with the F.A. Cup in the bag as well as a place in Europe. What was to follow was even more sensational, the Blues coming to within an ace of a remarkable treble. They won the League Championship and the European Cup Winners Cup before losing to Manchester United in the F.A. Cup Final.

Injury had kept Gray on the sidelines when the campaign started and the magnificent form of Sharp and Heath effectively kept him there until the beginning of December when Heath collected a terrible injury playing against Sheffield Wednesday. Andy said: 'No one could stop Graeme and Adrian in those early weeks as the side moved to the top of the League.

'They had played so well together that when 'Inchy' was injured, many people thought that the team's form might suffer and that Graeme and I might struggle as a partnership. But the run of League and Cup matches we put together gives me as much satisfaction as anything I've ever done.'

Gray singles out the Cup Winners Cup semi-final, second leg against Bayern Munich as the most exciting game he has ever played in. He said: 'I will never play in another match like it. It was 0-0 after the first leg in Germany and close on 50,000 people packed Goodison for the return. We went one down in the first half, but I knew we would get back.

'Graeme Sharp got the equaliser from a long throw and the place erupted. As soon as that went in, I looked at the opposition and could see them visibly cracking. I grabbed the equaliser and with the noise still thundering around Goodison, Trevor Steven finished them off.

'As we were walking down the tunnel at the end, Bayern's Uli Hoeness turned to me and said 'That was not football. You are all crazy men'. We had bombed them and it was a fantastic feeling. We knew that we were making history by becoming the first Everton side to reach a European final. We knew that the eleven who started the final against Rapid Vienna would never be forgotten.

'And just as we had been so confident in beating Watford in the F.A. Cup Final the previous season, we knew we would win in Rotterdam.'

F

Cup joy . . . Andy Gray holds the F.A. Cup watched by Gary Stevens in 1984.

Win they did and only sheer exhaustion — both mental and physical — prevented them from retaining the F.A. Cup at the expense of Manchester United. Andy Gray was to be sold during the close season when Everton bought Leicester City's Gary Lineker. The Scot's departure to Aston Villa was mourned by the Goodison faithful who sent petitions to manager Howard Kendall to record their bitter disappointment.

Andy said: 'I never wanted to leave Goodison. After the season I'd had, I didn't imagine I might be starting off in the reserves. But the boss wanted to buy Lineker, rightly or wrongly. I honestly think wrongly.

'What he gave to them and what they lost was different. They gained an out-and-out goalscorer, but lost someone who could make other players believe in themselves. Graeme Sharp was asked to do things which didn't suit his game. When Gary left the following summer, Everton paired Heath and Sharp together again and won the League.

'You can read into that what you like. Gary scored 40 goals in the one season he was at Goodison, but the Blues failed to win a trophy. I like to think that when I was in the side, we were the complete team. Gary is a fantastic goal-scorer and in the right set-up he'll win lots of medals, but Everton built their success on team work.

'When Howard sold me, he said "I'm going to get slaughtered for this." I said 'No you won't. Just go out and batter Manchester United in the Charity Shield and they'll forgive you.' I knew the lads would beat United because it was only tiredness after the European final that beat us in the F.A. Cup. I would like to think that if you ran a poll and asked Evertonians who they would rather see in that blue number nine shirt, Gray or Lineker, then I would give Gary a good run for his money.'

Andy certainly left his mark on Goodison Park. He had walked in the illustrious footsteps of the Deans, Lawtons and Royles and earned his place in the Goodison Hall of Fame on merit.

Terry Darracott, Everton's assistant manager, told me a little story that sums up Gray's character perfectly. He said: 'When I was reserve coach, Andy was with me for about six games and he scored seven goals. The attitude he showed and his leadership qualities with the younger players was tremendous. When he left, I sent him a letter saying that I would never forget him.

'We played in a Central League game at Blackburn Rovers and Howard Kendall was there, watching the game with a view to bringing Andy back into the first team on the Saturday after injury. He scored two goals inside ten minutes and then went over on his ankle. Although it didn't look too serious. Howard got a message down to me to get him off.

'He didn't want to take any chances because he wanted the lad right for Saturday. I thought nothing of it, shouting to Andy, 'Give me a couple of minutes while I get the sub warmed up.' He scowled at the bench and said, 'What do you mean coming off? I'm on a hat-trick.'

'He meant it. We virtually had to drag him off. It was a great thing for me because if ever you were lost for words in any way, all you had to say to the younger players was 'Hey, there's the standard being set by the oldest professional in the club. He's an international, a first-team player, one of the top men in the League. That's the level of performance and attitude you must aim for.

'Andy Gray was a great player for Everton, there's no doubt about that.'

FULL INTERNATIONAL CAPS
(Scotland score given first in each case)

1976: Rumania 1-1, Switzerland 1-0.
1977: Finland 6-0, Czechoslovakia 0-2.
1979: Austria 2-3, Norway 3-2.
1980: Portugal 0-0, England (sub) 0-2.
1981: Sweden 1-0, Portugal 0-0, Israel (sub) 1-0, Northern Ireland 1-1.
1982: Sweden (sub) 2-0, Northern Ireland (sub) 0-0.
1983: Northern Ireland 0-0, Wales 2-0, England 0-2, Canada 3-0, Canada 2-0.
1985: Iceland 1-0.
Total: 20.

CHAPTER TWELVE

Neville Southall

In an age when soccer egos often soar higher than a Sky Televison satellite, Neville Southall is a breath of fresh air.

The Everton goalkeeper's views on football are refreshing, different and forthright. Neville is not into designer clothes or designer sports gear for that matter. But he is tailor-made for stopping shots and headers from all distances and all angles.

Goalkeeping masters like Gordon Banks and Pat Jennings have described the Welsh international as world-class. Evertonians, tongue-in-cheek, claim that he is much better than that.

The man himself just gets on with the job, saying: 'Some people believe life is all about money and glory. To me, it's all about happiness.'

He means it. Neville's idea of a good time is to extend training by half an hour or take his two Alsatian dogs for a walk. He revels in his work and often starts a game muddier than some players finish it because of the intensity of his pre-match work-out. He's certainly a distinctive figure, standing between the posts with his socks rolled down and pads showing, almost as if he didn't have time to get dressed properly.

He laughs off a suggestion that he's setting a whole new trend in designer-scruff, explaining: 'That's the way I train, so that's the way I play. It might look a bit scruffy, but people don't care if you've got your shirt hanging out or whatever, so long as you're doing your job. If we all went round looking the same, it would be boring.'

Neville may look casual, but there is nothing laid back about his approach to goalkeeping. He has broken the hearts of some of the game's greatest strikers with saves

No, it's not Adrian Heath testing Neville in a training session! It's a young fan, having fun trying to beat the best in the world.

that defy logic. The fact of the matter is that as well as having outstanding goalkeeping qualities, he also does his homework.

He leaves nothing to chance, even taking note of the type of ball opponents use. He said: 'There are three or four different makes used in the League. At one time there used to be five. Most people think a ball is a ball, but they definitely vary in speed and bounce. Sometimes you see a shot dip over a keeper into the back of the net.

'The fans shake their heads, but it doesn't go through anyone's mind that the keeper might not have been used to the flight of the ball. At the same time, certain gloves don't have the same grip because of the different coatings on the balls. I always train in advance with the make of ball we're going to use in a particular match.'

Neville's professionalism and his standing as a goalkeeper of the very highest class earned him the ultimate

accolade in May, 1985, when he was named Footballer of
the Year. All those years of hard work and dedication had
paid off.

As a schoolboy, Neville played for the Caernarfon
District side, both as a goalkeeper and a centre-half. His
great rival between the posts at that time was a youngster
by the name of Eddie Niedzwiecki, later to play for
Wrexham and Chelsea.

The Caernarfon Boys manager was very lucky indeed to
have two lads in his side who would eventually keep goal
for Wales. Neville soon shelved any thoughts about being
an outfield player to concentrate on goalkeeping. He
couldn't get enough of it, turning out for the school on
Saturday mornings, playing in the rough-and-tumble
atmosphere of the Welsh League in the afternoon and then
getting in a third weekend game with a local Sunday
League side.

They say practice makes perfect, but it doesn't always
follow. Many of Neville's school pals played alongside him
for the Llandudno Swifts, and because of the youth of the
side they were out of their depth in the Welsh League
which boasted some very experienced players.

It's hard to imagine Southall picking the ball out of the
back of his net 16 times in one game, but it happened on
one occasion. The memory brings a beaming smile to his
face: 'We were such a young side that we were regularly
hammered,' he says. 'It was just a good laugh. We didn't
expect anything and put it down to experience.'

The school side was more successful. Neville said: 'We
represented Wales in the finals of a National Five-A-Side
tournament at Wembley Arena. England, Scotland and
Northern Ireland were all represented. I remember saving
four penalties in one game and we lost 5-4.'

Such is life for a keeper. By now Neville was beginning
to think about his future. Having left school, he took a job
with the local council in Llandudno. It was an 'explosive'
start to his working career. He had to help blow up and
knock down a number of gun emplacements which had

Top man . . . Andy Gray congratulates Neville Southall following the 1-0 League victory over arch-rivals Liverpool in May, 1985.

been built during the war to deal with any German planes heading towards Liverpool.

Neville's next challenge came at 'The Ritz' — not the famous establishment in London, but a cafe in Llandudno. He worked seven days a week for the princely sum of £18. Little wonder he jumped at an opportunity to work for a local builder as a hod carrier.

His employer would eventually become a millionaire. The only thing Neville got out of it was the sack and he found himself working as a bin-man in Llandudno. Labourer, cafe worker, hod carrier, bin man . . . it all seems a million light years away from the glamorous world of the professional footballer.

Neville looks back on it all philosophically, saying: 'Working on the bins and the like was never a problem. I was glad to do it. It was a job and you see a different side of life.'

All of the time he was working hard on his football. He played for Bangor City for a season, then Conwy United and finally Winsford. Whisper it quietly, but the only League football he used to watch at that time was at Old Trafford, the home of Manchester United.

He used to wait outside a pub to be picked up for the Winsford games and on the occasions when the matches were called off and his lift didn't arrive, he would go and stand at the Stretford End.

He said: 'I often wondered what it would be like out on the pitch. When I eventually ran out there as an Everton player, it was all a bit of a let down. It never seemed as good as you imagined it would be.'

Neville was producing some eye-catching performances for Winsford, even though he never used to train with his team-mates. He was having a second spell as a hod carrier and would arrive for matches in a somewhat haphazard manner, recalling: 'In one game, against Stalybridge Celtic, I didn't arrive until half-time because someone put a brick through the train window and it was delayed. It was 0-0 when I finally got there and we went on to lose 1-0. It's amusing looking back, but it wasn't very funny at the time.'

Bury saw fit to give the up-and-coming Southall a chance in the Football League. Neville said: 'I had an awful start. The fella who signed me on, Dave Connor, was sacked before the season even started. Jim Iley became boss and we never saw eye to eye, possibly because I was useless at first. But coach Wilf McGuiness, the former Manchester United boss, was tremendous. He took me for extra sessions in the afternoon. I had never had any special coaching before. Everything I did was instinctive — or luck!

'I remember that the crowd used to boo me when I first arrived. The previous keeper had been there for 14 years. We went bottom of the League after losing 2-1 to Wigan,

Footballer of the Year in 1985 . . . Howard Kendall congratulates the Everton keeper after the awards ceremony at the Savoy Hotel, London.

but I kept my place and we started to have a good run. There was a lot of talk about different Bury players going here, there and everywhere. I picked up the Sunday papers to read that I was on my way to Everton.'

Neville went in to see Iley who told him that the deal could not be finalised because Winsford were claiming 25 per cent of the £150,000 fee. The keeper was disappointed, but he was happy at Bury and took that as some consolation. Fortunately for the Blues, Howard Kendall was determined to get his man. Winsford finally agreed to accept £25,000. That suited Bury and Southall was on his way.

But the story took another twist when he headed for Rodney Street in Liverpool to take the medical. 'It was at the time of the Toxteth riots,' recalls Neville. 'Buildings were on fire just up the road. Like everyone else, I had heard different stories about the city. On one occasion, some of the lads had tyres nicked from their cars during a non-League game at South Liverpool!'

Nev decided that nothing was going to deflect him from his ambition to get to the top, not even a riot. He signed as Kendall moved in the market for a host of new players including the likes of Alan Biley, Mick Ferguson, Alan Ainscow and Mike Walsh.

Southall thought initially that he would be rivalling Jim McDonagh and Martin Hodge for the goalkeeping slot, but Kendall pulled a surprise when he went back to his old club, Blackburn Rovers, to capture Jim Arnold who went straight into the first team.

Arnold and Southall would battle it out with each other for the next two years, the Welsh keeper admitting: 'I learned a lot from Jim. He was a totally different person to me, but he had a good sense of humour and thought a lot about the game and how a goalkeeper should train.'

Neville made his first-team debut in a 2-1 victory over Ipswich on October 17, 1981. He made way for Arnold for the following seven games, but was then able to embark on a 25-match run that effectively made him Everton's number one going into the 1982/83 campaign.

International boss Mike England had been following the keeper's progress and on May 27, 1982, Neville made his debut for Wales against Northern Ireland.

It was in a Home International Championship clash at Wrexham. Ironically, he replaced former Everton stalwart Dai Davies who — at the age of 34 — had won his 50th cap for Wales a few days earlier.

But just when everything seemed to be going right for the keeper, Jim Arnold returned as Everton's first choice. The Blues were struggling for form and consistency at the start of that 82/83 campaign. Disaster struck early in the November when Liverpool arrived at Goodison to plunder a sensational 5-0 victory, Ian Rush claiming four. It was a disastrous day in every sense, on-loan defender Glenn Keeley getting sent off in his one and only game for the Blues.

It was always going to be a gamble playing the Blackburn Rovers centre-back who was short on match practice.

Everything under control . . . Neville puts a foot on the ball and surveys his domain at Goodison.

His dismissal left Everton's ten men with little or no chance against a rampant Liverpool and the day was to prove costly for the unfortunate Southall in every sense.

Kendall restored Arnold to the side for the following match at Arsenal, a 1-1 draw. When Jim kept four clean sheets in the next five games, it was clear that Neville was going to have to prove himself all over again.

Friends and enemies . . . Neville with ace Liverpool striker Ian Rush who once put four goals past him at Goodison. The pair, of course, are international team-mates.

The respect between the keepers was there for all to see. Neville was left out for 25 games in the wake of that Liverpool disaster, but played in the final four matches of that topsy-turvy 82/83 season in which the Blues finished a disappointing seventh.

Jim was back in the driving seat when the new season dawned, but Neville returned after seven matches and has effectively been Everton's number one ever since. It's now history that the Blues won the F.A. Cup that year after losing out in a fiercely contested Milk Cup Final replay to Liverpool. The Championship came to Goodison the

Two Everton giants . . . Neville and his former team-mate Peter Reid.
They dominated the votes in the 1985 Footballer of the Year poll.

following season for the first time in 15 years and Everton
won their first European trophy, the Cup Winners Cup.

Neville had played as big a part as anyone in the great
Goodison revival. People still talk about the save he made
at Spurs in that 1985 title-winning season.

A dozen games remained when Everton travelled to
White Hart Lane for an absolutely crucial contest. The
Blues were top, but Tottenham still fanced their chances. It
was to be a tremendous battle, the Blues leading 2-1 with
two minutes to go thanks to Andy Gray and Trevor Steven.
Mark Falco suddenly bulleted a header towards the roof of
the visitors' net and it looked a goal all the way until
Southall somehow tipped it over the top.

The Spurs boss at that time was Peter Shreeves. He said:
'The talk in our dressing room was all about the save near
the end that stopped us getting a draw. It was world class.'

The victory left Kendall's young lions four points clear at

the top and strengthened their grip on the most intriguing Championship for years. Neville's interpretation of the save, not unexpectedly, is typically modest. He says: 'Everyone went on about it, but it was more or less straight at me. When you're going for a title and it's an important game, things sometimes look better than they are.

'People overlook the unorthodox saves you make with your legs or your knees.' Asked to explain, he recalls a stop he made against Oxford on the way to the Milk Cup Final. Manager Howard Kendall was under a lot of pressure at that time and there had been calls for both his resignation and that of chairman Philip Carter just a couple of months earlier. Neville said: 'A shot came up and hit me on the knee, sailing up and over the bar. I look on that as a good save, because it could have been curtains if it had gone in.

'No one remembers it, but it was an important one for me. I don't think about particular incidents too much. The time to look back is when your youngster is old enough to sit on your knee and ask you about it.'

Neville has known despair as well as total elation. He suffered severe dislocation of the ankle and ligament damage playing for Wales against the Republic of Ireland in March, 1986. The injury was so acute that many people wondered if he would ever be able to get back to his brilliant best.

The man himself had no doubts. He said: 'I thought to myself, "You can't do anything else. You've got to fight back".

'My first reaction when it happened was "You stupid dope. You've broken your leg". Then I saw my ankle twisted the other way and I thought "Thank God for that, it's only the ankle".

'It's funny what goes through your mind. I even asked the doctor if I could shower before I went to the hospital. I took my own gear off when I got there after the nurse had cut my boot off. The worse thing was when the students came round to have a look at me!'

Making a young fan
feel at home at
Bellefield. Neville
takes time out from
training.

Even in his darkest hour, Neville was totally positive. He said: 'I never doubted that I would get back. I told myself that I had done nothing in life and got nothing. If I had to retire, would I be back to pushing a broom?

'John Clinkard, our physio at that time, did a tremendous job for me.'

Bobby Mimms played well in Neville's absence, playing in the F.A. Cup Final against Liverpool and the Charity Shield. Manager Kendall faced a tricky selection decision 15 games into the 1986/87 season. Southall had been out for seven months, but he was plunged into the home game against Watford and played a key role in another Championship success.

Looking back on his time at Goodison, Neville pinpoints that historic all-Merseyside Milk Cup Final against Liverpool as being all-important. He said: 'We proved at Wembley that we could match them.'

The big keeper admits to being 'gutted' about the replay defeat, not so much for himself as for the young Evertonians in the crowd who were in tears on the final whistle.

Neville said: 'We came of age together than night. We have had some proud moments, not least the night when we beat Rapid Vienna to win the Cup Winners Cup. We were right on song in that game. I can remember looking up the field and thinking, "Hey, we're not a bad side!"

'We have achieved all our success as a squad of lads with no individual taking all the glory. That's the way it should be.'

That may be the case, but no-one would underestimate the important contribution Neville has made down the years. Pat Jennings, one of Britain's greatest ever goalkeepers, has no doubts about Neville's standing as the Football League's current number one.

He said: 'He doesn't seem to have any weaknesses. He's brave, agile, has got good hands and gets on with the job. There is no doubt in my mind that of lot of Everton's success has been down to Nev. I couldn't pick anyone ahead of him in the country.'

Enough said!

FULL INTERNATIONAL CAPS
(Wales score given first in each case)

1982: Northern Ireland 3-0.

1983: Norway 1-0, England 1-2, Bulgaria 1-0, Scotland 0-2, Northern Ireland 1-0, Brazil 1-1.

1984: Norway 0-0, Rumania 5-0, Bulgaria 0-1, Yugoslavia 1-1, Scotland 1-2, England 1-0, Northern Ireland 1-1, Norway 0-1, Israel 0-0.

1985: Iceland 0-1, Spain 0-3, Iceland 2-1, Norway 1-1, Scotland 1-0, Spain 3-0, Norway 2-4.
1986: Scotland 1-1, Hungary 0-3, Saudi Arabia 2-1, Eire 1-0.
1987: Russia 0-0, Finland 4-0, Czechoslovakia 1-1.
1988: Denmark 1-0, Czechoslovakia 0-2, Yugoslavia 1-2, Sweden 1-4, Holland 1-0, Finland 2-2.
1989: Sweden 0-2, West Germany 0-0.
Total: 38.

* Up to May 1989.

Football League Record
1888-89 to 1988-89

		HOME					AWAY						
Season	P	W	D	L	F	A	W	D	L	F	A	Pts	Pos

FOOTBALL LEAGUE

Season	P	W	D	L	F	A	W	D	L	F	A	Pts	Pos
1888-89	22	8	0	3	23	14	1	2	8	12	32	20	8th
1889-90	22	8	2	1	40	15	6	1	4	25	25	31	2nd
1890-91	22	9	0	2	39	12	5	1	5	24	17	29	1st
1891-92	26	8	2	3	32	22	4	2	7	17	27	28	5th

FIRST DIVISION

Season	P	W	D	L	F	A	W	D	L	F	A	Pts	Pos
1892-93	30	9	3	3	44	17	7	1	7	30	34	36	3rd
1893-94	30	11	1	3	63	23	4	2	9	27	34	33	6th
1894-95	30	12	2	1	47	18	6	4	5	35	32	42	2nd
1895-96	30	10	4	1	40	17	6	3	6	26	26	39	3rd
1896-97	30	8	1	6	42	29	6	2	7	20	28	31	7th
1897-98	30	11	3	1	33	12	2	6	7	15	27	35	4th
1898-99	34	10	2	5	25	13	5	6	6	23	28	38	4th
1899/1900	34	11	1	5	30	15	2	6	9	17	34	33	11th
1900-01	34	10	4	3	37	17	6	1	10	18	25	37	7th
1901-02	34	11	2	4	31	11	6	5	6	22	24	41	2nd
1902-03	34	10	2	5	28	18	3	4	10	17	29	32	12th
1903-04	34	13	0	4	36	12	6	5	6	23	20	43	3rd
1904-05	34	14	2	1	36	11	7	3	7	27	25	47	2nd
1905-06	38	12	1	6	44	30	3	6	10	26	36	37	11th
1906-07	38	16	2	1	50	10	4	3	12	20	36	45	3rd
1907-08	38	11	4	4	34	24	4	2	13	24	40	36	11th
1908-09	38	11	3	5	51	28	7	7	5	31	29	46	2nd
1909-10	38	8	6	5	30	28	8	2	9	21	28	40	10th
1910-11	38	12	3	4	34	17	7	4	8	16	19	45	4th
1911-12	38	13	5	1	29	12	7	1	11	17	30	46	2nd
1912-13	38	8	2	9	28	31	7	5	7	20	23	37	11th
1913-14	38	8	7	4	32	18	4	4	11	14	37	35	15th
1914-15	38	8	5	6	44	29	11	3	5	32	18	46	1st
1919-20	42	8	6	7	42	29	4	8	9	27	39	38	16th
1920-21	42	9	8	4	40	26	8	5	8	26	29	47	7th
1921-22	42	10	7	4	42	22	2	5	14	15	33	36	20th
1922-23	42	14	4	3	41	20	6	3	12	22	39	47	5th
1923-24	42	13	7	1	43	18	5	6	10	19	35	49	7th
1924-25	42	11	4	6	25	20	1	7	13	15	40	35	17th

		HOME					AWAY						
Season	P	W	D	L	F	A	W	D	L	F	A	Pts	Pos
1925-26	42	9	9	3	42	26	3	9	9	30	44	42	11th
1926-27	42	10	6	5	35	30	2	4	15	29	60	34	20th
1927-28	42	11	8	2	60	28	9	5	7	42	38	53	1st
1928-29	42	11	2	8	38	31	6	2	13	25	44	38	18th
1929-30	42	6	7	8	48	46	6	4	11	32	46	35	22nd
SECOND DIVISION													
1930-31	42	18	1	2	76	31	10	4	7	45	35	61	1st
FIRST DIVISION													
1931-32	42	18	0	3	84	30	8	4	9	32	34	56	1st
1932-33	42	13	6	2	54	24	3	3	15	27	50	41	11th
1933-34	42	9	7	5	38	27	3	9	9	24	36	40	14th
1934-35	42	14	5	2	64	32	2	7	12	25	56	44	8th
1935-36	42	12	5	4	61	31	1	8	12	28	58	39	16th
1936-37	42	12	7	2	56	23	2	2	17	25	55	37	17th
1937-38	42	11	5	5	54	34	5	2	14	25	41	39	14th
1938-39	42	17	3	1	60	18	10	2	9	28	34	59	1st
1946-47	42	13	5	3	40	24	4	4	13	22	43	43	10th
1947-48	42	10	2	9	30	26	7	4	10	22	40	40	14th
1948-49	42	12	5	4	33	25	1	6	14	8	38	37	18th
1949-50	42	6	8	7	24	20	4	6	11	18	46	34	18th
1950-51	42	7	5	9	26	35	5	3	13	22	51	32	22nd
SECOND DIVISION													
1951-52	42	12	5	4	42	25	5	5	11	22	33	44	7th
1952-53	42	9	8	4	38	23	3	6	12	33	52	38	16th
1953-54	42	13	6	2	55	27	7	10	4	37	31	56	2nd
FIRST DIVISION													
1954-55	42	9	6	6	32	24	7	4	10	30	44	42	11th
1955-56	42	11	5	5	37	29	4	5	12	18	40	40	15th
1956-57	42	10	5	6	34	28	4	5	12	27	51	38	15th
1957-58	42	5	9	7	34	35	8	2	11	31	40	37	16th
1958-59	42	11	3	7	39	38	6	1	14	32	49	38	16th
1959-60	42	13	3	5	50	30	0	8	13	23	58	37	16th
1960-61	42	13	4	4	47	23	9	2	10	40	46	50	5th
1961-62	42	17	2	2	64	21	3	9	9	24	33	51	4th
1962-63	42	14	7	0	48	17	11	4	6	36	25	61	1st
1963-64	42	14	4	3	53	26	7	6	8	31	38	52	3rd
1964-65	42	9	10	2	37	22	8	5	8	32	38	49	4th
1965-66	42	12	6	3	39	19	3	5	13	17	43	41	11th
1966-67	42	11	4	6	39	22	8	6	7	26	24	48	6th
1967-68	42	18	1	2	43	13	5	5	11	24	27	52	5th
1968-69	42	14	5	2	43	10	7	10	4	34	26	57	3rd

Season	P	W	D	L	F	A	W	D	L	F	A	Pts	Pos
1969-70	42	17	3	1	46	19	12	5	4	26	15	66	1st
1970-71	42	10	7	4	32	16	2	6	13	22	44	37	14th
1971-72	42	8	9	4	28	17	1	9	11	9	31	36	15th
1972-73	42	9	5	7	27	21	4	6	11	14	28	37	17th
1973-74	42	12	7	2	29	14	4	5	12	21	34	44	7th
1974-75	42	10	9	2	33	19	6	9	6	23	23	50	4th
1975-76	42	10	7	4	37	24	5	5	11	23	42	42	11th
1976-77	42	9	7	5	35	24	5	7	9	27	40	42	9th
1977-78	42	14	4	3	47	22	8	7	6	29	23	55	3rd
1978-79	42	12	7	2	32	17	5	10	6	20	23	51	4th
1979-80	42	7	7	7	28	25	2	10	9	15	26	35	19th
1980-81	42	8	6	7	32	25	5	4	12	23	33	36	15th
1981-82	42	11	7	3	33	21	6	6	9	23	29	64	8th
1982-83	42	13	6	2	43	19	5	4	12	23	29	64	7th
1983-84	42	9	9	3	21	12	7	5	9	23	30	62	7th
1984-85	42	16	3	2	58	17	12	3	6	30	26	90	1st
1985-86	42	16	3	2	54	18	10	5	6	33	23	85	2nd
1986-87	42	16	4	1	49	11	10	4	7	27	20	86	1st
1987-88	40	14	4	2	34	11	5	9	6	19	16	70	4th
1988-89	38	10	7	2	33	18	4	5	10	17	27	54	8th

Post War F.A. Cup Record

1946-47	Round 3	Southend United	(h)	4-2
	Round 4	Sheffield Wednesday	(a)	1-2
1947-48	Round 3	Grimsby Town	(a)	4-1
	Round 4	Wolverhampton Wanderers	(a)	1-1
	(Replay)	Wolverhampton Wanderers	(h)	3-2
	Round 5	Fulham	(a)	1-1
	(Replay)	Fulham	(h)	0-1
1948-49	Round 3	Manchester City	(h)	1-0
	Round 4	Chelsea	(a)	0-2
1949-50	Round 3	Queens Park Rangers	(a)	2-0
	Round 4	West Ham United	(a)	2-1
	Round 5	Tottenham Hotspur	(h)	1-0
	Round 6	Derby County	(a)	2-1
	Semi Final	Liverpool (Maine Road)		0-2
1950-51	Round 3	Hull City	(a)	0-2
1951-52	Round 3	Leyton Orient	(a)	0-0
	(Replay)	Leyton Orient	(h)	1-3
1952-53	Round 3	Ipswich Town	(h)	3-2
	Round 4	Nottingham Forest	(h)	4-1
	Round 5	Manchester United	(h)	2-1
	Round 6	Aston Villa	(a)	1-0
	Semi Final	Bolton Wanderers (Maine Road)		3-4

Post War F.A. Cup Record (cont'd)

1953-54	Round 3	Notts County	(h)	2-1
	Round 4	Swansea Town	(h)	3-0
	Round 5	Sheffield Wednesday	(a)	1-3
1954-55	Round 3	Southend United	(h)	3-1
	Round 4	Liverpool	(h)	0-4
1955-56	Round 3	Bristol City	(h)	3-1
	Round 4	Port Vale	(a)	3-2
	Round 5	Chelsea	(h)	1-0
	Round 6	Manchester City	(a)	1-2
1956-57	Round 3	Blackburn Rovers	(h)	1-0
	Round 4	West Ham United	(h)	2-1
	Round 5	Manchester United	(a7	0-1
1957-58	Round 3	Sunderland	(a)	2-2
	(Replay)	Sunderland	(h)	3-1
	Round 4	Blackburn Rovers	(h)	1-2
1958-59	Round 3	Sunderland	(h)	4-0
	Round 4	Charlton Athletic	(a)	2-2
	(Replay)	Charlton Athletic	(h)	4-1
	Round 5	Aston Villa	(h)	1-4
1959-60	Round 3	Bradford City	(a)	0-3
1960-61	Round 3	Sheffield United	(h)	0-1
1961-62	Round 3	King's Lynn	(h)	4-0
	Round 4	Manchester City	(h)	2-0
	Round 5	Burnley	(a)	1-3
1962-63	Round 3	Barnsley	(a)	3-0
	Round 4	Swindon Town	(a)	5-1
	Round 5	West Ham United	(a)	0-1
1963-64	Round 3	Hull City	(a)	1-1
	(Replay)	Hull City	(h)	2-1
	Round 4	Leeds United	(a)	1-1
	(Replay)	Leeds United	(h)	2-0
	Round 5	Sunderland	(a)	1-3
1964-65	Round 3	Sheffield Wednesday	(a)	2-2
	(Replay)	Sheffield Wednesday	(a)	3-0
	Round 4	Leeds United	(a)	1-1
	(Replay)	Leeds United	(h)	1-2

Post War F.A. Cup Record (Cont'd)

1965-66	Round 3	Sunderland	(h)	3-0
	Round 4	Bedford Town	(a)	3-0
	Round 5	Coventry City	(h)	3-0
	Round 6	Manchester City	(a)	0-0
	(Replay)	Manchester City	(h)	0-0
	(Replay 2)	Manchester City (Molineux)		2-0
	Semi Final	Manchester United	1-0	
		(Burnden Park)		
	Final	Sheffield Wednesday		3-2
		(Wembley)		
1966-67	Round 3	Burnley	(a)	0-0
	(Replay)	Burnley	(h)	2-1
	Round 4	Wolverhampton Wanderers	(a)	1-1
	(Replay)	Wolverhampton Wanderers	(h)	3-1
	Round 5	Liverpool	(h)	1-0
	Round 6	Nottingham Forest	(a)	2-3
1967-68	Round 3	Southport	(a)	1-0
	Round 4	Carlisle United	(a)	2-0
	Round 5	Tranmere Rovers	(h)	2-0
	Round 6	Leicester City	(a)	3-1
	Semi Final	Leeds United		1-0
		(Old Trafford)		
	Final	West Bromich Albion		0-1
		(Wembley)		
1968-69	Round 3	Ipswich Town	(h)	2-1
	Round 4	Coventry City	(h)	2-0
	Round 5	Bristol City	(h)	1-0
	Round 6	Manchester United	(a)	1-0
	Semi Final	Manchester City		0-1
		(Villa Park)		
1969-70	Round 3	Sheffield United	(a)	1-2
1970-71	Round 3	Blackburn Rovers	(h)	2-0
	Round 4	Middlesbrough	(h)	3-0
	Round 5	Derby County	(h)	1-0
	Round 6	Colchester United	(h)	5-0
	Semi Final	Liverpool		1-2
		(Old Trafford)		
1971-72	Round 3	Crystal Palace	(a)	2-2
	(Replay)	Crystal Palace	(h)	3-2
	Round 4	Walsall	(h)	2-1
	Round 5	Tottenham Hotspur	(h)	0-2

Post War F.A. Cup Record (cont'd)

1972-73	Round 3	Aston Villa	(h)	3-2
	Round 4	Millwall	(h)	0-2
1973-74	Round 3	Blackburn Rovers	(h)	3-0
	Round 4	West Bromich Albion	(h)	0-0
	(Replay)	West Bromich Albion	(a)	0-1
1974-75	Round 3	Altrincham	(h)	1-1
	(Replay)	Altrincham	(a)	2-0
		(at Old Trafford)		
	Round 4	Plymouth Argyle	(a)	3-1
	Round 5	Fulham	(h)	1-2
1975-76	Round 3	Derby County	(a)	1-2
1976-77	Round 3	Stoke City	(h)	2-0
	Round 4	Swindon Town	(a)	2-2
	(Replay)	Swindon Town	(h)	2-1
	Round 5	Cardiff City	(a)	2-1
	Round 6	Derby County	(h)	2-0
	Semi Final	Liverpool (Maine Road)		2-2
	(Replay)	Liverpool (Maine Road)		0-3
1977-78	Round 3	Aston Villa	(h)	4-1
	Round 4	Middlesbrough	(a)	2-3
1978-79	Round 3	Sunderland	(a)	1-2
1979-80	Round 3	Aldershot	(h)	4-1
	Round 4	Wigan Athletic	(h)	3-0
	Round 5	Wrexham	(h)	5-2
	Round 6	Ipswich Town	(h)	2-1
	Semi Final	West Ham United		1-1
		(Villa Park)		
	(Replay)	West Ham United		1-2
		(Elland Road)		
1980-81	Round 3	Arsenal	(h)	2-0
	Round 4	Liverpool	(h)	2-1
	Round 5	Southampton	(a)	0-0
	(Replay)	Southampton	(h)	1-0
	Round 6	Manchester City	(h)	2-2
	(Replay)	Manchester City	(a)	1-3
1981-82	Round 3	West Ham United	(a)	1-2
1982-83	Round 3	Newport County	(a)	1-1
	(Replay)	Newport County	(h)	2-1
	Round 4	Shrewsbury Town	(h)	2-1
	Round 5	Tottenham Hotspur	(h)	2-0
	Round 6	Manchester United	(a)	0-1

Post War F.A. Cup Record (Cont'd)

1983-84	Round 3	Stoke City	(a)	2-0
	Round 4	Gillingham	(h)	0-0
	(Replay)	Gillingham	(a)	0-0
	(Replay 2)	Gillingham	(a)	3-0
	Round 5	Shrewsbury Town	(h)	3-0
	Round 6	Notts County	(a)	2-1
	Semi Final	Southampton (Highbury)		1-0
	Final	Watford (Wembley)		2-0
1984-85	Round 3	Leeds United	(a)	2-0
	Round 4	Doncaster Rovers	(h)	2-0
	Round 5	Telford United	(h)	3-0
	Round 6	Ipswich Town	(h)	2-2
	(Replay)	Ipswich Town	(a)	1-0
	Semi Final	Luton Town (Villa Park)		2-1
	Final	Manchester United (Wembley)		0-1
1985-86	Round 3	Exeter City	(h)	1-0
	Round 4	Blackburn Rovers	(h)	3-1
	Round 5	Tottenham Hotspur	(a)	2-1
	Round 6	Luton Town	(a)	2-2
	(Replay)	Luton Town	(h)	1-0
	Semi Final	Sheffield Wednesday (Villa Park)		2-1
	Final	Liverpool (Wembley)		1-3
1986-87	Round 3	Southampton	(h)	2-1
	Round 4	Bradford City	(a)	1-0
	Round 5	Wimbledon	(a)	1-3
1987-88	Round 3	Sheffield Wednesday	(a)	1-1
	(Replay)	Sheffield Wednesday	(h)	1-1
	(Replay 2)	Sheffield Wednesday	(h)	1-1
	(Replay 3)	Sheffield Wednesday	(a)	5-0
	Round 4	Middlesbrough	(h)	1-1
	(Replay)	Middlesbrough	(a)	2-2
	(Replay 2)	Middlesbrough	(h)	2-1
	Round 5	Liverpool	(h)	0-1
1988-89	Round 3	West Bromich Albion	(a)	1-1
	(Replay)	West Bromich Albion	(h)	1-0
	Round 4	Plymouth Argyle	(a)	1-1
	(Replay)	Plymouth Argyle	(h)	4-0
	Round 5	Barnsley	(a)	1-0

Post War F.A. Cup Record (cont'd)

Round 6	Wimbledon	(h)	1-0
Semi Final	Norwich City (Villa Park)		1-0
Final	Liverpool (Wembley)		2-3

F.A. Charity Shield

1928	Blackburn Rovers (Old Trafford)		2-1
1932	Newcastle United	(a)	5-3
1933	Arsenal	(h)	0-3
1963	Manchester United	(h)	4-0
1966	Liverpool	(h)	0-1
1970	Chelsea	(a)	2-1
1984	Liverpool (Wembley)		1-0
1985	Manchester United (Wembley)		2-0
1986	Liverpool (Wembley)		1-1
1987	Coventry City (Wembley)		1-0

League Cup Record

1960-61	Round 1	Accrington Stanley	(h)	3-1
	Round 2	Walsall	(h)	3-1
	Round 3	Bury	(h)	3-1
	Round 4	Tranmere Rovers	(a)	4-0
	Round 5	Shrewsbury Rovers	(a)	1-2
* Did not enter for next six seasons				
1967-68	Round 2	Bristol City	(a)	5-0
	Round 3	Sunderland	(h)	2-3
1968-69	Round 2	Tranmere Rovers	(h)	4-0
	Round 3	Luton Town	(h)	5-1
	Round 4	Derby County	(h)	0-0
	(Replay)	Derby County	(a)	0-1
1969-70	Round 2	Darlington	(a)	1-0
	Round 3	Arsenal	(a)	0-0
	(Replay)	Arsenal	(h)	1-0
	Round 4	Manchester City	(a)	0-2
* Did not enter 1970-71				
1971-72	Round 2	Southampton	(a)	1-2
1972-73	Round 2	Arsenal	(a)	0-1
1973-74	Round 2	Reading	(h)	1-0
	Round 3	Norwich City	(h)	0-1
1974-75	Round 2	Aston Villa	(a)	1-1
	(Replay)	Aston Villa	(h)	0-3

League Cup Record (cont'd)

1975-76	Round 2	Arsenal	(h)	2-2
	(Replay)	Arsenal	(a)	1-0
	Round 3	Carlisle United	(h)	2-0
	Round 4	Notts County	(h)	2-2
	(Replay)	Notts County	(a)	0-2
1976-77	Round 2	Cambridge United	(h)	3-0
	Round 3	Stockport County	(a)	1-0
	Round 4	Coventry City	(h)	3-0
	Round 5	Manchester United	(a)	3-0
	Semi Final	Bolton Wanderers	(h)	1-1
	Semi Final	Bolton Wanderers	(a)	1-0
	Final	Aston Villa (Wembley)		0-0
	(Replay)	Aston Villa (Hillsborough)		1-1
	(Replay 2)	Aston Villa (Old Trafford)		2-3
1977-78	Round 2	Sheffield United	(a)	3-0
	Round 3	Middlesbrough	(h)	2-2
	(Replay)	Middlesbrough	(a)	2-1
	Round 4	Sheffield Wednesday	(a)	3-1
	Round 5	Leeds United	(a)	1-4
1978-79	Round 2	Wimbledon	(h)	8-0
	Round 3	Darlington	(h)	1-0
	Round 4	Nottingham Forest	(h)	2-3
1979-80	Round 2/1	Cardiff City	(h)	2-0
	Round 2/2	Cardiff City	(a)	0-1
	Round 3	Aston Villa	(a)	0-0
	(Replay)	Aston Villa	(h)	4-1
	Round 4	Grimsby Town	(a)	1-2
1980-81	Round 2/1	Blackpool	(h)	3-0
	Round 2/2	Blackpool	(a)	2-2
	Round 3	West Bromich Albion	(h)	1-2
1981-82	Round 2/1	Coventry City	(h)	1-1
	Round 2/2	Coventry City	(a)	1-0
	Round 3	Oxford United	(h)	1-0
	Round 4	Ipswich Town	(h)	2-3
1982-83	Round 2/1	Newport County	(a)	2-0
	Round 2/2	Newport County	(h)	2-2
	Round 3	Arsenal	(h)	1-1
	(Replay)	Arsenal	(a)	0-3
1983-84	Round 2/1	Chesterfield	(a)	1-0
	Round 2/2	Chesterfield	(h)	2-2

League Cup Record (cont'd)

	Round 3	Coventry City	(h)	2-1
	Round 4	West Ham United	(a)	2-2
	(Replay)	West Ham United	(h)	2-0
	Round 5	Oxford United	(a)	1-1
	(Replay)	Oxford United .	(h)	4-1
	Semi Final	Aston Villa	(h)	2-0
	Semi Final	Aston Villa	(a)	0-1
	Final	Liverpool (Wembley)		0-0
	Final	Liverpool (Maine Road)		0-1
1984-85	Round 2/1	Sheffield United	(a)	2-2
	Round 2/2	Sheffield United	(h)	4-0
	Round 3	Manchester United	(a)	2-1
	Round 4	Grimsby Town	(h)	0-1
1985-86	Round 2/1	Bournemouth	(h)	3-2
	Round 2/2	Bournemouth	(a)	2-0
	Round 3	Shrewsbury Town	(a)	4-1
	Round 4	Chelsea	(a)	2-2
	(Replay)	Chelsea	(h)	1-2
1986-87	Round 2/1	Newport County	(h)	4-0
	Round 2/2	Newport County	(a)	5-1
	Round 3	Sheffield Wednesday	(h)	4-0
	Round 4	Norwich City	(a)	4-1
	Round 5	Liverpool	(h)	0-1
1987-88	Round 2/1	Rotherham United	(h)	3-2
	Round 2/2	Rotherham United	(a)	0-0
	Round 3	Liverpool	(a)	1-0
	Round 4	Oldham Athletic	(h)	2-1
	Round 5	Manchester City	(h)	2-0
	Semi Final	Arsenal	(h)	0-1
	Semi Final	Arsenal	(a)	1-3
1988-89	Round 2/1	Bury	(h)	3-0
	Round 2/2	Bury	(a)	2-2
	Round 3	Oldham Athletic	(h)	1-1
	(Replay)	Oldham Athletic	(a)	2-0
	Round 4	Bradford City	(a)	1-3

* Competition was known as the Milk Cup between 1981/82 and 1985/86. Subsequently called the Littlewoods Cup.

European Cup
1963-64 Round 1 (1) Inter Milan (h) 0-0
Round 1 (2) Inter Milan (a) 0-1
(aggregate 0-1)
1970-71 Round 1 (1) Keflavik (h) 6-2
Round 1 (2) Keflavik (a) 3-0
(aggregate 9-2)
Round 2 (1) Borussia Möenchengladbach (a) 1-1
Round 2 (2) Borussia Möenchengladbach (h) 1-1
(aggregate 2-2
Everton won 4-3 on penalties)
Round 3 (1) Panathinaikos (h) 1-1
Round 3 (2) Panathinaikos (a) 0-0
(aggregate 1-1
Panathinaikos won on away goals)

European Cup-Winners' Cup
1966-67 Round 1 (1) Aalborg (a) 0-0
Round 2 (1) Aalborg (h) 2-1
(aggregate 2-1)
Round 2 (1) Real Zaragoza (a) 0-2
Round 2 (2) Real Zaragoza (h) 1-0
(aggregate 1-2)
1984-85 Round 1 (1) UC Dublin (a) 0-0
Round 1 (2) UC Dublin (h) 1-0
(aggregate 1-0)
Round 2 (1) Bratislava (a) 1-0
Round 2 (2) Bratislava (h) 3-0
(aggregate 4-0)
Round 3 (1) Fortuna Sittard (h) 3-0
Round 2 (2) Fortuna Sittard (a) 2-0
(aggregate 5-0)
Semi (1) Bayern Munich (a) 0-0
Semi (2) Bayern Munich (h) 3-1
(aggregate 3-1)
Final Rapid Vienna 3-1
(at Rotterdam)

Inter-Cities Fairs' Cup
1962-63 Round 1 (1) Dunfermline Athletic (h) 1-0
Round 1 (2) Dunfermline Athletic (a) 0-2
(aggregate 1-2)

Inter-Cities Fairs' Cup (cont'd)

1964-65	Round 1 (1)	Valerengen	(a)	5-2
	Round 1 (2)	Valerengen	(h)	4-2
			(aggregate 9-4)	
	Round 2 (1)	Kilmarnock	(a)	2-0
	Round 2 (2)	Kilmarnock	(h)	4-1
			(aggregate 6-1)	
	Round 3 (1)	Manchester United	(a)	1-1
	Round 3 (2)	Manchester United	(h)	1-2
			(aggregate 2-3)	
1965-66	Round 1 (1)	IFC Nuremberg	(a)	1-1
	Round 1 (2)	IFC Nuremberg	(h)	1-0
			(aggregate 2-1)	
	Round 2 (1)	Ujpest Dosza	(a)	0-3
	Round 2 (2)	Ujpest Dosza	(h)	2-1
			(aggregate 2-4)	

UEFA Cup

1975-76	Round 1 (1)	AC Milan	(h)	0-0
	Round 1 (2)	AC Milan	(a)	0-1
			(aggregate 0-1)	
1978-79	Round 1 (1)	Finn Harps	(a)	5-0
	Round 1 (2)	Finn Harps	(h)	5-0
			(aggregate 10-0)	
	Round 2 (1)	Dukla Prague	(h)	2-1
	Round 2 (2)	Dukla Prague	(a)	0-1
			(aggregate 2-2	
		Dukla Prague won on away goals)		
1979-80	Round 1 (1)	Feyenoord	(a)	0-1
	Round 1 (2)	Feyenoord	(h)	0-1
			(aggregate 0-2)	

Final Teams — F.A. Cup
1892-93
Mar 25 v Wolverhampton Wanderers (Fallowfield) 0-1
Williams, Howarth, Kelso, Stewart, Holt, Boyle, Latta, Gordon, Maxwell, Chadwick, Milward.
1896-97
Apr 10 v Aston Villa (Crystal Palace) 2-3 (Bell, Boyle)
Menham, Meecham, Storrier, Boyle, Holt, Stewart, Taylor, Bell, Hartley, Chadwick, Milward.

Final Teams — F.A. Cup (cont'd)
1905-06
Apr 21 v Newcastle United (Crystal Palace) 1-0 (Young)
Scott, W. Balmer, Crelly, Makepeace, Taylor, Abbott, Sharp,
Bolton, Young, Settle, H.P. Hardman.
1906-07
Apr 20 v Sheffield Wednesday (Crystal Palace) 1-2 (Sharp)
Scott, W. Balmer, R. Balmer, Makepeace, Taylor, Abbott,
Sharp, Bolton, Young, Settle, H.P. Hardman.
1932-33
Apr 29 v Manchester City (Wembley) 3-0 (Stein, Dean, Dunn)
Sagar, Cook, Cresswell, Britton, White, Thomson, Geldard,
Dunn, Dean, Johnston, Stein.
1965-66
May 14 v Sheffield Wednesday (Wembley) 3-2 (Trebilcock 2,
Temple)
West, Wright, Wilson, Gabriel, Labone, Harris, Scott, Trebil-
cock, Young, Harvey, Temple.
1967-68
May 18 v West Bromich Albion (Wembley) 0-1
West, Wright, Wilson, Kendall, Labone, Harvey, Husband, Ball,
Royle, Hurst, Morrissey.
1983-84
May 19 v Watford (Wembley) 2-0 (Sharp, Gray)
Southall, Stevens, Bailey, Ratcliffe, Mountfield, Reid, Steven,
Heath, Sharp, Gray, Richardson.
1984-85
May 18 v Manchester United (Wembley) 0-1
Southall, Stevens, Van den Hauwe, Ratcliffe, Mountfield, Reid,
Steven, Gray, Sharp, Bracewell, Sheedy.
1985-86
May 10 v Liverpool (Wembley) 1-3 (Lineker)
Mimms, Stevens (Heath), Van den Hauwe, Ratcliffe, Mountfield,
Reid, Steven, Lineker, Sharp, Bracewell, Sheedy.

Football League Cup
1976-77
Mar 12 v Aston Villa (Wembley) 0-0
Lawson, Jones, Darracott, Lyons, McNaught, King, Hamilton,
Dobson, Latchford, McKenzie, Goodlass.

Football League Cup (cont'd)
Apr 13 v Aston Villa (second replay) (Old Trafford) 2-3 (Latchford, Lyons)
Lawson, Robinson, Darracott, Lyons, McNaught, King, Hamilton, Dobson, Latchford, Pearson (Sargeant), Goodlass.
1983-84
Mar 25 v Liverpool (Wembley) 0-0.
Southall, Stevens, Bailey, Ratcliffe, Mountfield, Irvine, Heath, Sharp, Richardson, Sheedy (Harper).
Mar 28 v Liverpool (replay) (Maine Road) 0-1
Southall, Stevens, Bailey, Ratcliffe, Mountfield, Reid, Irvine (King), Heath, Sharp, Richardson, Harper.

European Cup-Winners' Cup
1984-85
May 15 v Rapid Vienna (Rotterdam) 3-1 (Gray, Sheedy, Steven)
Southall, Stevens, Van den Hauwe, Ratcliffe, Mountfield, Reid, Steven, Sharp, Gray, Bracewell, Sheedy.